cutting edge Photo cropping

for scrapbooks, book 2

wave chaser

Joshua

Laguna Beach

The boys love being on their boards
so much that they will endure the
often chilly Pacific Ocean for hours

MEMORY
MAKERS
BOOKS

Executive Editor Kerry Arquette   **Founder** Michele Gerbrandt

Senior Editor MaryJo Regier

Art Director Andrea Zocchi

Designer Nick Nyffeler

Craft Editor Jodi Amidei

Art Acquisitions Editor Janetta Wieneke

Photographer Ken Trujillo

Contributing Photographers Marc Creedon, Brenda Martinez

Contributing Writers Kelly Angard, Nicole Cummings

Editorial Support Emily Curry Hitchingham, Dena Twinem

Hand Model Ann Kitayama

Featured Artists See *Artist Index* on page 121

Memory Makers® Cutting Edge Photo Cropping for Scrapbooks Book 2
Copyright © 2003 Memory Makers Books
All rights reserved.

Published by Memory Makers Books, an imprint of F+W Publications, Inc.
4700 East Galbraith Road, Cincinnati, OH 45236
Phone 1-800-289-0963
First edition. Printed in the United States of America.
11 10 09 08 07 9 8 7 6 5

Library of Congress Cataloging-in-Publication Data

Cutting edge photo cropping for scrapbooks.
    p. cm.
  Includes bibliographical references and index.
  ISBN-13: 978-1-892127-24-2 (pbk. : alk. paper)
  ISBN-10: 1-892127-24-5 (pbk. : alk. paper)
   1. Photographs--Trimming, mounting, etc. 2. Photograph albums 3. Scrapbooks I.
  Memory makers.

  TR340.C88 2003
  771'.46--dc21

2003056208

Memory Makers Books is the home of Memory Makers, the scrapbook magazine dedicated to educating and inspiring scrapbookers. Visit us on the Internet at www.memorymakersmagazine.com.

this book belongs to:

We dedicate this book to all of our *Memory Makers* contributors
who aspire to experiment and fall in love with creative photo cropping as we have.

"Though we travel the world over
to find the beautiful,
we must carry it with us
or we find it not."

Ralph Waldo Emerson

introduction

Our photos are the heart and soul of our scrapbooks, and thousands of scrapbookers and photo enthusiasts have discovered the joy of creative photo cropping. If you are hungry for new photo-cropping ideas, we are excited to provide more innovative ways to communicate using your photos. As you experiment with and explore this special niche of scrapbooking, you will learn that there are many ways you can use a single photograph. Conversely, there are certain photos that just beg for a specific type of photo cropping.

To answer every need, we feature dozens of ideas in this book—from simple to complex—all equally intriguing and inspiring. The first chapter includes brand-new ideas for cropping photos into slices and segments and mats and frames. It also introduces the art of photo tearing. The next chapter explores never-before-seen ways to crop photos using shapes—from tags and template shapes to letters, symbols and punched shapes.

The final chapter reveals innovative ways to showcase photo weaving, mosaics and collage, and ends with whimsical ways to bring movement to your photos. Easy-to-follow instructions and illustrated step shots make these photo projects appealing and doable. As always, we recommend that you work with duplicates (see page 10) and not your original photos. Or, at least have a negative on file for backup. The use of photo-safe paper and adhesives will help ensure the longevity of your photo art.

Our goal with this book is to inspire you to push your photo cropping beyond the boundaries of traditional scrapbooking. We hope you enjoy this fresh generation of cutting edge cropping techniques sure to trigger personal, highly individualized results with your own images. Take a few minutes to sharpen those scissors, put a new blade in your craft knife and let the creativity begin!

Michele

Michele Gerbrandt
Founding Editor
Memory Makers magazine

getting started

Photo "cropping" or cutting begins with photographs. Famed photographer Ansel Adams once said, "Twelve significant photos in any one year is a good crop." Mr. Adams was a bit more discerning than the average picture-taker. He had a keen eye for cropping photos through the lens with breathtaking results. Today's savvy scrapbookers are creating quality photos with the added indulgence of physically cropping a photographic print to manipulate its composition for eye-pleasing effects.

when to crop

A photo can tell many stories depending on how it is cropped. As you experiment with photo cropping, you will become keenly aware of what types of photo cropping techniques work best for certain types of photo compositions. And for those photo blunders, photo cropping allows you to remedy the situation in many cases. Put creative photo cropping to use in the following situations for eye-pleasing results:

Command Focus

Busy photos, with lots of people and unnecessary background, take attention away from the photos' subjects. Framing, slicing and silhouetting can isolate and focus attention on your subject.

Correct Flaws

Cropping allows you to remove photo blemishes, such as flare from flashes, closed eyes, strangers in your pictures, out-of-focus elements, lab printing errors and more. It even allows you to use "junk" photos from the beginning of a roll of film!

Boost Style

Add style and variety to your page by cropping your photos into a shape. There are many shapes with which to experiment, and changing the shape will also change the final effect. Give your cropped photo breathing room, however, so that the photo's content is not lost.

Design New Art

Herein lies the reason behind this book and the allure of creative photo cropping—the "shear" fun and enjoyment of cropping a photo into a new piece of photo art.

Using Photo Scraps

Save your photo scraps and snippets as you are cropping. Most will be reassembled back into the new piece of art but you can also use photo scraps to create custom-coordinated photo frames (see page 34), put in photo shaker boxes (see page 53), make "illuminated" lettering (see page 67) or title letters (see page 114), form interesting borders (see page 74) or a mini mosaic (see page 100), incorporate into a photo collage (see page 103) or use for matting journaling blocks (see page 107).

when not to crop

As entertaining as photo cropping can be, there are some types of photos that should not be cropped. Before you begin cropping, keep these tips in mind:

Heritage Photos

Consider the value to future generations if one-of-a-kind family heirloom or other old photographs are left intact. Crop duplicates of historic photos instead of cropping the originals.

Artistic Photos

Cropping can minimize the artistic composition of a photograph. Perhaps the photographer's out-of-focus foreground lends a perspective that would be lost if you cut it out. Maybe the extra space around the subject was deliberately composed to evoke a certain mood. Before cropping, consider the drama of a photo's imagery.

Polaroid Prints

A Polaroid "integral" print (above; noted for its thickness and ¾" lower white border) should not be cropped. The positive and negative sides of the print stay together, and cutting the print exposes the chemical layers. Instead of cutting an integral print, use a color copy of the print for cropping.

Polaroid "peel apart" photos (above) are safe to crop. The final print is separated from the reactive chemicals and the negative when the photo is peeled apart.

Photo and Negative Handling and Storage

Photo cropping relies on ordering reprints and enlargements from negatives or photos. Use these tips for easy access and preservation of photos and negatives:

- Wash and dry hands before handling negatives, then wear cotton gloves to prevent scratching the negatives.
- Avoid cutting negative strips, which ruins the emulsion and the negative.
- Keep negatives and photos organized chronologically or by subject or theme for quick access.
- Prior to ordering reprints, clean negatives with a commercial-grade emulsion cleaner, such as PEC-12® (Photographic Solutions).
- Use 100 percent acid-, lignin- and PVC-free negative sleeves, storage binders and storage boxes.
- If storing negatives in an acid-free envelope, separate strips with acid-free paper to prevent sticking.
- Store away from dust, bright light and excessive heat or high humidity; store in temperatures between 65-70 degrees with 30-50 percent humidity.
- Store negatives separately from photos, ideally in a safe-deposit box.

photo duplication

The easiest way to duplicate your photos is by having reprints or enlargements made from your negatives. However, we often have photos for which we have no negatives. Fortunately, there are ways to duplicate photos without the use of negatives.

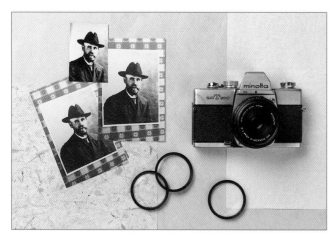

Color Copy Machines

The least expensive duplication option is to use a laser color copier, which is sensitive to the different shades in photographs. Color copiers allow you to change the size of the image. For preservation purposes, use acid-free, 28-pound or heavier, smooth white paper. Color photocopy toner is known to be more stable than inkjet dyes, so choose color copying over printing with an inkjet printer when possible. In addition, use a mat or other barrier between layered photos and color copies of photos when possible. Color copy machines can be found at select scrapbook stores or office supply stores.

Take a Picture of a Picture

The biggest benefit of this method is that it creates negatives for your photos. A manual 35mm SLR camera—with an inexpensive, close-up or macro lens set—works great for this purpose. Simply place your photo on a flat surface or tape it to a wall in bright, even light, then focus and snap!

Digital Photo Machines

Digital, print-to-print photocopy machines (shown is Kodak's Picture Maker) are user-friendly, self-service machines that can be found at your local discount, photography, drug store or supermarket. Some popular standard features include the ability to make enlargements and reductions, custom cropping, rotating and zooming in, and the ability to sharpen and adjust color and brightness of images. Some allow you to convert a color print to a black-and-white or sepia-toned photo. Many digital photo machines have the ability to write images to floppy disks and print from CD-ROMS.

KODAK Picture CD and KODAK Picture Maker are registered trademarks of © Eastman Kodak Company, 2003. Used with permission.

Scanning Photos or Printing Digital Images

To scan your photos at home, use the TIFF file format for high-resolution images. The quality of your duplicated photos will depend on the quality of your scanner, scanning software, printer and the photo paper you print on (shown is Epson's Glossy Photo Paper made specifically for scrapbooking). If do-it-yourself scanning is not for you, you can have high quality photo scans put on a CD-ROM at a camera store, mini lab or professional lab. To print images from a CD-ROM, a high-quality color printer and photo-quality printer paper will give the best color results.

cropping tools & supplies

The tools listed below are used time and time again throughout this book to create photo art. Little extras, such as acid-neutralizing wipes for hands and photo fingerprint and adhesive cleaner, keep photos in quality condition before and after cropping. An embossing stylus or photo-safe wax pencil can be used for tracing cutting lines onto photos. Use a fine-grained sandpaper nail file, with a light and careful touch, to smooth cropped, curved photo edges.

Cropping Essentials

- Acid-neutralizing hand wipes
- Craft knife
- Cutting mat
- Embossing stylus
- Fine-grained sandpaper nail file
- Graphing ruler
- Metal straightedge ruler
- Paper trimmer
- Photo fingerprint and adhesive cleaner
- Photo-safe wax pencil
- Small, sharp scissors

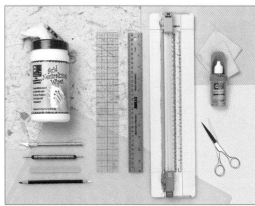

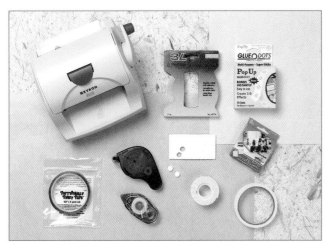

Photo-Safe Adhesives

We recommend the use of archival-quality adhesives for mounting your new photo art onto acid- and lignin-free paper and scrapbook pages. The adhesives most widely used are:

- Adhesive application machine
- Double-sided photo tape
- Glue sticky circles
- Photo tab mounting squares
- Removable artist's tape
- Repositionable adhesive dots
- Self-adhesive foam spacers
- Self-adhesive foam tape
- Tape runner
- Terrifically Tacky Tape™

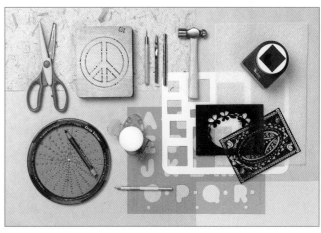

Additional Cropping Tools

The following items are used randomly throughout this book to complete specific photo-cropping techniques. In many cases, you may apply or substitute a specific tool that you already have on hand for one used in a given project.

- Decorative scissors
- Dies
- Eyelet-setting tools
- Foam core board (not shown)
- Piercing tool or sewing needle
- Plastic foam cutting mat
- Punches
- PVC-free page protectors (not shown)
- Shape cutters
- Swivel-blade craft knife
- Templates

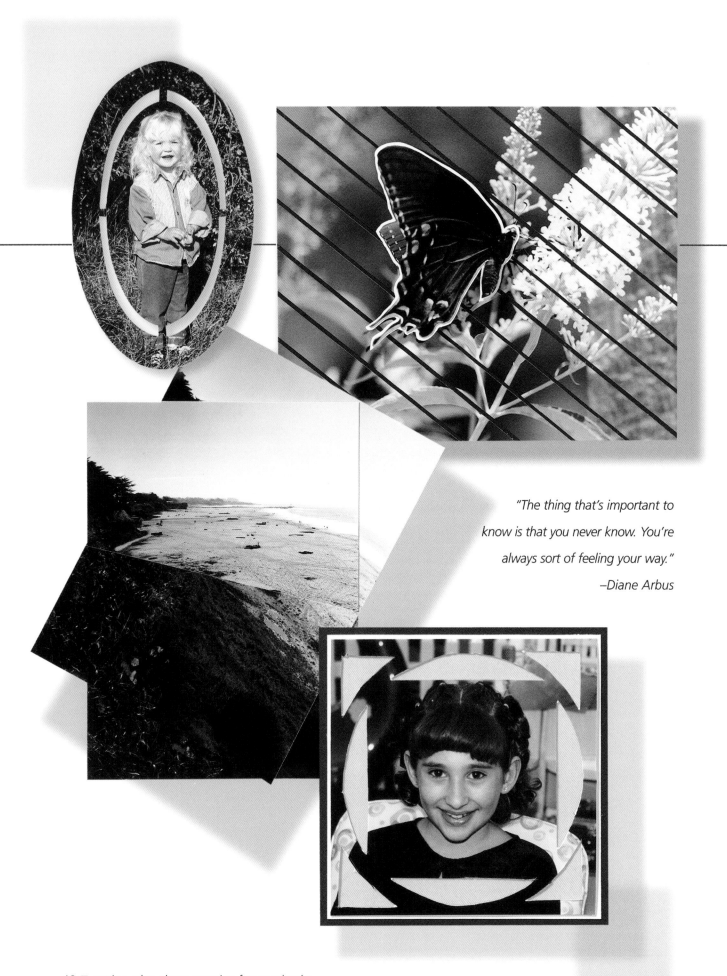

"The thing that's important to know is that you never know. You're always sort of feeling your way."
–Diane Arbus

basic cropping

It's amazing how the most fundamental cropping techniques can bring dazzling results to your photo art. With a few little cuts here and a few snips there, your photos will take on a whole new look. Some of the things you will learn in this chapter include how to:

- Cut and reassemble slices for interesting effects
- Combine vertical and diagonal slices for visual appeal
- Layer silhouettes atop slices for impact
- Combine vertical and horizontal slices with photo segments
- Slice oval- or circle-cropped photos into new art
- Curve panoramic photos to fit an 8½ x 11" page
- Slice slots for inserting photo accents
- Curl slices to create movement
- Slice reverse-image photos to create reflections
- Create sliced photo under- and overlays
- Frame mini photos with cropped photos
- Use partial silhouetting for a degree of separation
- Cut a foam core photo shadowbox
- Crop a self-framing photo shaker box
- Pierce and shadow-cut self-framing photos
- Tear photos in a number of ways for amazing aftereffects

These fresh and basic photo-cropping techniques are guaranteed to spark a creative fire with easy-to-achieve outcomes. Once you feel comfortable with these basic yet striking ideas, you'll feel empowered to bring more of your scrapbook tools and supplies into use to crop photos creatively.

slices & segments

All you need is a sharp craft knife and a metal straightedge ruler to crop photos into slices and segments. The strategic placement of your cropped slices and segments is what gives your photos flair when reassembled. Watch for straight lines in photo images; they provide obvious and natural cutting lines. Or, experiment by cropping random slices and segments across photos for a unique surprise upon reassembly!

Slice horizontally on a vertical panorama

Kelly Angard (Highlands Ranch, Colorado) brings focus to her son by cutting random-sized slices into a vertical panoramic photo. Use removable artist's tape to hold photo down onto cutting mat. Cut slices into photo with a craft knife and metal straightedge ruler. Assemble slices, leaving even spaces between the slices, and mount onto page. Try this simple vertical-slice technique on a horizontal panoramic photo for the same framing effect.

Offset a sliced corner

Jodi Amidei (Memory Makers) gives an interesting twist to a photo framing effect. First, slice the right or left corner from a vertical photo using a craft knife and metal straightedge ruler. Reassemble the picture onto your page, offsetting the cropped corner at an angle. Experiment with slicing both the upper right and lower left corners from a horizontal picture and reassembling onto the page at opposite angles for a more dramatic effect. Photo Kelli Noto (Centennial, Colorado)

Stack corner photo slices

Cutting the corners from duplicate photos is a clever technique that Melanie Fischer (Centennial, Colorado) uses to make this cool pool layout. To start, remove a ⅛" wide inset corner from your original photo. Continue by slicing ⅛" wide corners from the duplicate photos, making smaller corners as you go. Stack the corner slices on your layout by mounting away from your center photo, mounting the slices from largest to smallest. This technique pulls your eyes into the focal point of the layout—the photo subject.

Slice randomly and reassemble

Take some great photos, add an eye-pleasing photo cropping technique, and you get a fabulous layout like this one by Kelly Angard (Highlands Ranch, Colorado). When cutting your own pictures, keep a pattern to your slices. For example, crop ¼" slices on one picture, ½" slices on another and combine the two measurements to crop ¾" slices on yet another photo. Slices can be vertical or horizontal, based on the position of the subject in the photo, as long as the slices leave the main photo subject intact. Reassemble slices on page with even spacing for added drama. Photos Jeff Neal (Huntington Beach, California)

Combine offset vertical with diagonal slices

To make this visually pleasing frame that focuses on the majesty of her pet, Karen Wilson-Bonnar (Pleasanton, California) combined vertical offset segments at one end of her photo with diagonal slices at the other end. Keeping the diagonal slices at just one end of the photo helps draw the eye through the entire picture. Crop the vertical slices in random sizes and assemble and mount offset onto page. Assemble and mount diagonal slices onto page leaving even spaces between the slices.

Combine different photos to impact horizon

When Sue Nunamaker (Villa Park, Illinois) made a mistake on a photo she cropped for a layout, she unwittingly stumbled upon a new photo-cropping technique. Sue placed the slices of a miscropped photo onto a similar, uncut photo and realized the neat effect it had. To accomplish this technique, gather two photos with similar horizons. Use removable artist's tape to hold one photo down to a cutting mat. Crop ⅜" slices from the photo with a metal straightedge ruler and craft knife. Mount the slices ¼" apart on the uncut photo. This technique would be a beautiful way to enhance photos of grassy hills, snowy mountainsides and other gorgeous landscape shots. The key is to use a background photo that is very similar to the sliced photo, yet different enough in color to see the difference between the two.

Couple horizontal and vertical slices

Brandi Ginn (Lafayette, Colorado) uses a combination of horizontal and vertical slices on two different photos to give the illusion that they are one, while using the same effect to frame a picture mounted on a tag. Use removable artist's tape to hold photos down onto cutting mat while cropping ½" slices with a metal straightedge ruler and craft knife. Assemble slices onto page leaving space between each slice while placing photos directly next to each other. For a twist on the tag, cut horizontal slices from parts of a photo to frame the photo subject and mirror the cropping technique on the page. Photos Brian Cummings (Aliso Creek, California)

Join vertical- and diagonal-sliced photos

The visual impact of this technique comes from the placement of the diagonal photo slices. To do this, Jodi Amidei (Memory Makers) used a photo of a flowering tree, sliced it vertically and then joined it with a diagonally sliced photo of a sports car. The slices are alternated when reassembled onto the page. Crop the right and left side of the first photo into ⅛" slices. Cut the rest of the photo into ¼" slices. Follow the same measurements when cutting a second photo, only this time cut diagonally. Assemble, alternating slices from both photos onto page, first with a temporary adhesive then permanently when satisfied with the arrangement. Photos Erica Pierovich (Longmont, Colorado)

Shredding Photos

Put that handy little office appliance, the paper shredder, to use cropping photo slices for you. If desired, first apply adhesive to the back of the photo with an adhesive application machine. After shredding, some assembly will be required.

1 To crop a photo into vertical or horizontal slices, feed either the photo's vertical or horizontal straight edge into the shredder.

2 To crop a photo into diagonal slices, hold the photo by one corner and feed the opposite corner into the shredder.

Combine diagonal segments with silhouette

Silhouetting gives any picture interest and "popping" the silhouette adds to the spectacle. To add drama to this silhouette-cropped butterfly, Jodi Amidei (Memory Makers) sliced diagonal lines in the original picture for a dazzling background. Begin with two copies of the same photo. Mount first photo to a cutting mat with removable artist's tape and crop photo into ⅜" diagonal slices with a craft knife and metal straightedge ruler. Silhouette crop the subject from the second photo as shown and mat on white cardstock. Assemble slices evenly spaced on a piece of cardstock. Trim the photo-laden cardstock with a paper trimmer to a smaller size so it is "borderless." Apply the silhouette-cropped image atop its original image on the first photo, using self-adhesive foam spacers for lift. This technique works well for page layouts as well as the cover piece for handmade cards.

1 Use small, sharp scissors to silhouette crop around contours of the photo subject. Cut slowly, following each outline, being careful not to lob off any necessary features. Use a sharp craft knife to crop around tiny parts that are not easily accessible with scissors.

Accent horizontal slices with crimped silhouette

Using a crimper on a silhouette-cropped American Flag, Diana Hudson (Bakersfield, California) gives the flag a very realistic look—as if it is waving in the wind. Slice a background photo into equal segments to break up the pattern of the sparks for a wavy look. Adhere the crimped and silhouette-cropped flag with self-adhesive foam spacers over the slices. For variation, try crimping the background segments also.

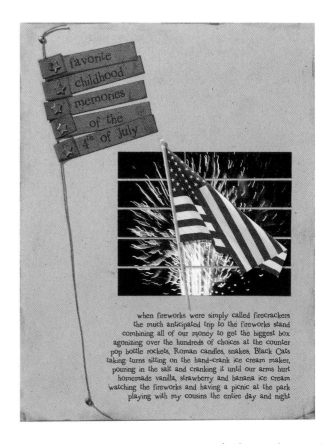

Mix random vertical slices with linear segments

Using slices and segments together is what Heidi Schueller (Waukesha, Wisconsin) did with a hot air balloon picture. First, use a photo-safe wax pencil and graphing ruler to mark the cutting lines for slices and segments onto photo. This will allow you to experiment with how you would like to showcase the highlights of the photo by simply wiping off misplaced lines. When satisfied with the look, crop the slices and segments with a craft knife and metal straight-edge ruler, wiping off the wax pencil residue as you go. Assemble on page like a mosaic—leaving spaces in between the slices and segments. Try this technique on garden, travel and architectural photos, making slices and segments around key elements of the photos' subjects.

Combine random horizontal slices with linear segments

Cutting random horizontal slices into bowling photos gives Heidi Schueller (Waukesha, Wisconsin) the result she was looking for—the illusion that the bowling ball is breaking apart the photos wherever it hits. Mark cutting lines and "cut-in" depths with a graphing ruler and photo-safe wax pencil. Tack photos onto cutting mat with removable artist's tape. Use a metal straightedge ruler and craft knife to slice on the marked lines, adding a diagonal cut at each end. Wipe off any pencil residue with a soft cloth. Reassemble and mount photos on layout, pulling slices out randomly for a jagged look.

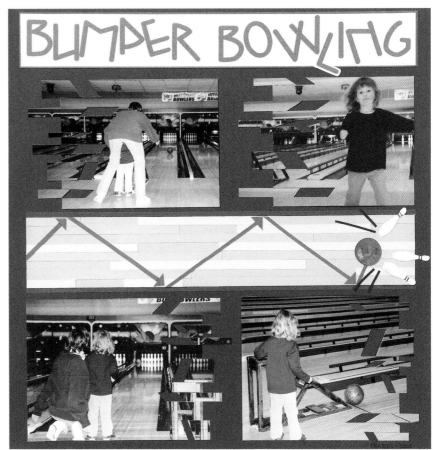

Add variety to circle- or oval-cropped photos

Slicing a casual pattern into circle- or oval-cropped photos adds visual impact to these fun-filled amusement park photos of Kelly Angard (Highlands Ranch, Colorado) with her daughter. Start with a circle- or oval-cropped photo. Follow the step below to crop slices. For variation, experiment with different slicing patterns as shown in the illustrations. Reassemble and mount slices on brightly colored cardstock, if desired.

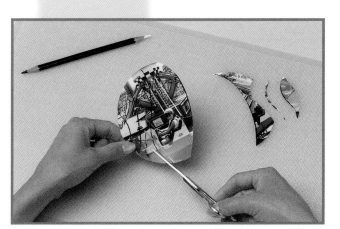

1 Use a photo-safe wax pencil to freehand draw random cutting lines on photo. Use small, sharp scissors or a craft knife to cut on the cutting lines. Use a soft cloth to wipe off any pencil residue from photo slices.

Sean, Cameron & Amber Stutzman
Maui - July 2000

Curve a panoramic photo

Some photos, such as these Maui panoramas, deserve to be showcased in a unique way.
But panoramas can be hard to fit on an 8½ x 11" page layout. Jodi Amidei (Memory Makers)
made an interesting layout by slicing and visually "curving" the photos upon reassembly.
This technique is unique in that it mimics the effect of a "fish eye" camera lens and you feel as
though you are out there on a boat yourself. Follow the instructions on the next page to apply
this technique to panoramic photos. Inspiration Corinne Cullen Hawkins (Walnut Creek,
California); Photos Pennie Stutzman (Broomfield, Colorado)

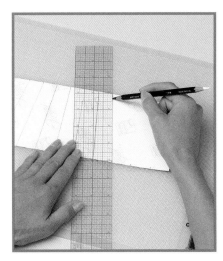

1 Flip photos over. Along the lower edge of the bottom photo, use a graphing ruler and a pencil to make "tick marks" at 1" intervals, beginning at the photo's center and working outward. Along the upper edge of the photo, make tick marks at ¾" intervals, beginning at the center and working outward. Use a pencil to connect the upper and lower marks (shown) to create the cutting lines, starting with a vertical line at the center and working outward. Repeat this step for your top photo, this time making ¾" interval tick marks on lower edge and 1" interval tick marks on upper edge of photo.

2 Use a craft knife and metal straightedge ruler to slice on the cutting lines, keeping photo slices in order for easier reassembly. Repeat this step for top photo.

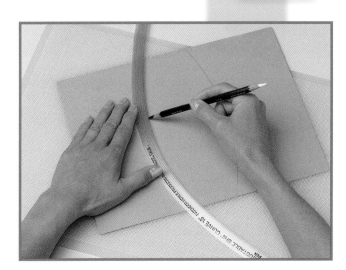

3 Measure up 4½" from lower edge of 8½ x 11" inch cardstock background and make tick marks on both the right and left sides of the cardstock at this point. Place a curve ruler (Hoyle) on these two points, allowing the ruler to curve slightly down in the center. Use a pencil to draw a slight curve to serve as a placement guideline for reassembling the photo slices. Rotate the cardstock 90 degrees and repeat this step on the top of the cardstock for the top photo.

4 Reassemble the lower photo slices, beginning with the center slice placed directly at the center, working from the center outward. Use a removable adhesive (Hermafix) in case you need to pick up a slice for better placement. When reassembling, overlap photo slices slightly on upper edges to help form the curve, picking up and replacing slices as needed. Repeat this step with top photo.

Insert page accents into sliced slots

Beverly Sizemore (Sulligent, Alabama) came up with an innovative way to accent a seaside photo. She replicated the sea grass in the photo, and inserted the grass into cropped slots in the foreground to make it look as though the grass was growing from the photo! Follow the step below to apply this technique. For variation, use a craft knife to slice the sides of individual grass blades directly on the photo, leaving a portion of the grass blades still connected to the photo (shown at right). Curl the sliced photo grass blades forward around a pencil to add dimension. Experiment with this technique on any photo that has easily replicated objects in the foreground or background, such as leaves, rocks, etc.

1 Use a craft knife to freehand cut short slots into the foreground at the base of the sea grass in the photo. Tuck freehand-cut paper sea grass into the slots and secure grass blades on the back of the photo with tape to hold in place.

Curl wavy slices for movement

Jodi Amidei (Memory Makers) applies an easy slicing technique to effectively mimic the rolling waves of the ocean in the photo. Secure the photo onto a cutting mat with removable artist's tape. Use a craft knife and a wavy ruler to slice the waves into the photo. Apply adhesive around the outside edges only of the photo and mount on page. After the adhesive is dry, use the tip of your craft knife to lift up the sliced edges and gently "roll" them forward. Apply liquid adhesive to the underside of the slices that stay in contact with the page for added firmness. Photo Leslie Aldridge (Broomfield, Colorado)

Slice half circles for spherical dimension

This serene photo of MaryJo Regier's (Memory Makers) three little seldom-serene boys bounces to life when half-circle slices are cut into the blown bubbles and curled forward slightly for a realistic look. MaryJo used a block-printing cutter (Speedball) with a curved, half-moon blade to puncture the photo strategically on one side of each bubble in the photo. This technique can be applied to any small, orb-shaped objects in photos—such as the balls in a ballroom, baseball or tennis balls in flight, a polka-dot dress or buttons on a shirt. Remember, the key to the realistic look is to curl the sliced half-circles forward slightly to shape.

Slice and curl to mimic waves

Kelly Angard (Highlands Ranch, Colorado) wanted to give the feel that you were right in the raft with her son. To accomplish this technique, flip photo over and mark a small "s" pattern repeatedly into the water portion of a photo with a wax pencil. Tape your photo onto a cutting mat with removable artist's tape and cut the "s" pattern with a craft knife. Turn photo over again and lift the cuts slightly, bending them gently forward. Mount photo on a watercolor background to accent the openings of the cuts. A variation on this technique is to cut random-sized "s" patterns into the water—making larger-sized patterns where the waves in the water are bigger, and smaller-sized patterns where the waves are smaller.

Slice waves to imitate breeze

Slicing quick-and-easy waves across a photo can create the feeling of a breeze. Cynthia Anning (Virginia Beach, Virginia) used a wavy ruler and craft knife to slice across the upper and lower edges of this photo, highlighting the autumn fun of her active young son. Try this with any outdoor activity photos where wind or waves are part of the subject matter, whether real or imagined! Assemble slices to background paper, leaving space in between each segment.

Join scenic photos with random slices

Most scrapbook pages are made with photos, but Kathy Graham (Miamisburg, Ohio) made a travel album cover page from extra scenic photos that might have otherwise gone unused. For an 8½ x 11" layout, select 6-8 photos. Layer photos randomly on a cutting mat and rearrange until you are pleased with the new scene. Use a craft knife to freehand cut random slices into photos, using each previously cut photo as a visual pattern for cutting the next photo. Don't worry about not getting the slices to match perfectly; cutting imperfections here lend to the allure of the finished artwork. Cut into the finished art to accommodate paper-pieced art, if desired. Use a lettering template and additional photos or photo scraps to create a page title for extra pizazz.

Slice a reverse image to create a reflection

When a luxury liner came to port in her neighborhood, Alison Lindsay (Edinburgh, Scotland) had to go see it. Alison was so impressed with the ship that she wanted a dramatic visual effect to help convey that. Slicing a reverse image of the ship gave her just what she was looking for. To start, obtain a reverse-image reprint of your original photo. To get a reverse image, the photo print operator should flip the negative so that the emulsion side is opposite of the correct printing method normally used. Request that the original image and the reverse image are an exact match. Turn reverse-image photo upside down so top of ship is at bottom of photo. Use a wavy ruler and craft knife to crop photo into slices. Reassemble slices on page so that ship is upside down to create a reflection. This is a great mirroring effect that could be used for just about any photo, not necessarily just those around water.

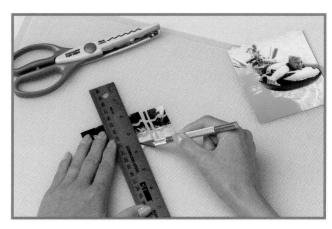

1 Crop slices in desired widths from edges of photo with decorative scissors. Reassemble slices and mount with temporary adhesive directly on cutting mat. Use a metal straightedge ruler and craft knife to crop ⅛" wide vertical segments from slices at 1" intervals; discard the small slices. Reassemble photo segments onto cardstock, lining up edges and leaving even spaces in between each segment.

Try decorative-scissor-sliced segments

Torrey Miller (Thornton, Colorado) shows a great new use for decorative scissors on this wet-and-wild photo. Follow the step above to use wave-patterned scissors (Fiskars) to slice segments that will draw your eye to a photo's focal point. Try this technique on any activity photos where a little implied movement is desired. For variation, try cropping vertically down the sides. Photo MaryJo Regier (Memory Makers)

Combine partial circles with random slices and segments

Cutting random slices and segments from an enlarged photo, and matting it the way Julie Mullison (Superior, Colorado) did, gives it the conceptual feel of looking into a stained-glass window. To apply this technique, pay special attention to where you are cutting and where you put your cut-out pieces so as not to "lose" them when reassembling the pieces back onto your cardstock. The illustrated steps below depict how to turn a photo into a stained-glass work of art.

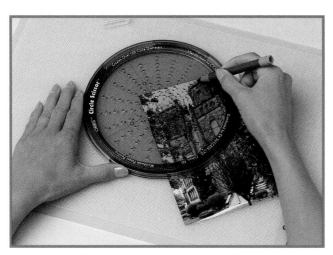

1 Use a circle scissor (EK Success), circle cutter or circle template to cut a partial or quarter circle from one corner of a photo.

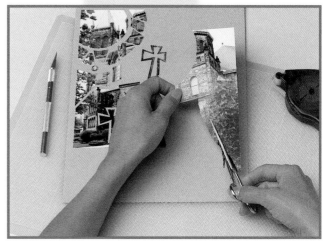

2 Mount partial circle on corner of cardstock. Use scissors or a craft knife to freehand slice or crop random slices and segments from the remainder of the photo, reassembling with temporary adhesive as you go. Use a craft knife to cut a theme-related symbol into the photo, if desired.

Interlock sliced half circles

Sometimes we design our pages to flow with our photos, like Trudy Sigurdson (Victoria, British Columbia, Canada) did in these pictures of her daughter playing in the wind. By cutting and tucking sliced half circles in the photos, Trudy re-created the feeling of movement depicted in the photo. First, use an adhesive application machine to apply lightweight, complementary-colored cardstock to back of photo. Follow the steps below to create photo art. To add visual contrast, mat finished photo art to a deeper shade of the same color cardstock.

1 Use a graduated circle template (Coluzzle® by Provo Craft) and a swivel craft knife or the outer edge of the brass stencil (Cut-N-Tuc® template by Stamporium) to crop the photo into a circle the same size as the outer edge of the brass stencil.

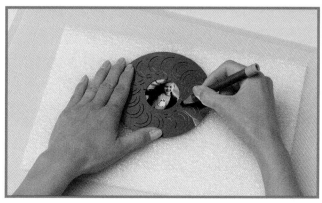

2 Place brass stencil atop circle-cropped photo; hold in place with removable artist's tape (3M), if desired. Use a craft knife to slice the photo, slicing through all slots or channels on the brass stencil.

3 Fold slices up and tuck behind each consecutive slice to form a ringed frame around the photo subject.

"Old hat,
NEW HAT..."

Michaela just loves hats! Seeing these pictures of her wearing all of her hats reminds of the Berenstain Bear book my mom used to read to me, "Old Hat, New Hat."

Slice and fold photo-framing accents

To add triangle accents to her photos, Julie Mullison (Superior, Colorado) used a template (Incire™ by Avec/Ecstasy Crafts) to cut them into her photos. To make the contrast in the slices, Julie used a yellow ink pad on the back of the pictures and then mounted them to purple cardstock after they were cut. Use a medium sandpaper to lightly sand the back of the picture to remove any of the photo's processing information and to hold the ink better. Secure your photo with removable adhesive and lay the template on the photo and center. Use a craft knife to slice through the template's slots or channels and the photo. Pull back gently on the sliced areas to expose the colored backing of the photo.

Crop a vertical-segment overlay

Kelli Noto (Centennial, Colorado) used vertically cut and overlaid photo segments to give a casual portrait added intrigue. Slice photo in half vertically. Cut 1" off the top of the left side of the photo, and 1" off the bottom of the right side of the photo. This will give the illusion that you have mounted them offset. Mat the cut photos to cardstock, lining up facial features in the portrait. Mount the right side of your photo directly onto your layout. Mount the left side with self-adhesive foam spacers.

Use horizontal segments for comparison

Holle Wiktorek (Clarksville, Tennessee) came up with an interesting way to compare the facial features of her family members. This technique would be a fun thing to do between siblings, parents, or even between close friends! Choose or take close-up photos of the people you want to compare features with. Make duplicate copies of your photos. Slice the photos into segments that feature just the eyes, noses or mouths in horizontal strips. Mount them by category and in the order the original photos appear on the page. Consider photographing and cropping other parts of the body as well—such as hands, feet, eyebrows or ears—for making amusing studies in genetic anatomy. Use this technique with photos of friends to accentuate differences and to identify possible similarities.

Separate segments with journaling

Try this simple yet engaging way to break up an image without losing the image's full content—separate the photo segments with journaling or page accents. By cutting her picture into segments and separating the segments, Trudy Sigurdson (Victoria, British Columbia, Canada) "lengthens" the photo and gives the illusion that this is a panoramic photo. Slice vertical photo into three to four segments and mount separated from each other. For variation, experiment with this technique on a horizontal photo.

Reassemble cut segments with eyelets

Kelly Angard (Highlands Ranch, Colorado) found a riveting technique that works great for photos with a lot of background. Kelly does a great job of keeping your eye on the boys, but makes the whole photo more playful by the way it's reassembled. Slice photo into equal or random segments, being careful not to cut through any faces or important objects in your photo. Number the pieces on the back for easier reassembly. Mount the pieces onto cardstock leaving space in between the segments. Set eyelets (see page 37) into the connecting corners of the segments. String paper yarn or fiber in a crisscross pattern through the eyelets and around the outer edges of the cardstock and secure from behind with tape.

Slice a duplicate to make an over- and underlay

Jodi Amidei (Memory Makers) uses an over- and underlay technique with two different colors of the same photo to give all new angles to the original photo. Start with one color and one black-and-white copy of the same photo. Lay the black-and-white photo on a cutting mat and secure with removable artist's tape. Make a diagonal cut with a craft knife and metal straightedge ruler all the way across the photo. Use a temporary adhesive to mount your original photo onto paper. Then, using the removable adhesive, experiment with the way you want your black-and-white photo to lay under and over the original color photo. Once satisfied, mount in place with permanent adhesive. This technique also gives some great new angles when done with horizontal photos. Photo Bruce Aldridge (Broomfield, Colorado)

Alternate color with black-and-white photo segments

Combining color with segments of a duplicate black-and-white photo is a captivating way to make any layout more appealing. Ruthann Grabowski's (Yorktown, Virginia) cropping technique successfully keeps the emphasis on the boys in the photo while playing up the beauty of Pennsylvania countryside in the background. To create this effect, select a color photo with nice scenery in the background. Make a black-and-white duplicate of the photo. Layer photos together front to back and hold together with temporary adhesive. Use a metal straightedge ruler and craft knife to crop random, triangular segments across photo. Separate photo segments; wipe off any adhesive residue. Reassemble into original image, alternating color with black-and-white photo segments. Use remaining set of segments for a second piece of photo art ready-made for gift giving!

mats & frames

In and out of the scrapbooking realm, some photos just beg for special mat and frame treatments. What makes these captivating mats and frames so spectacular is that they're all made with photos. You may be so impressed with the final results that you'll be tempted to hang them in your home instead of tucking them away safely in a scrapbook!

> Time is made up of captured moments.
> The things shared and the moments spent
> together become gifts that the heart never forgets.
>
> - Author Unknown

Crop mini frames from spare photos

Mini photo frames are all the rage. So Trudy Sigurdson (Victoria, British Columbia, Canada) came up with the idea of making her own style of mini frames from spare photos! First, punch or cut a 3" square from spare photo. Use decorative scissors around the edges of the square for accent, if desired. Remove a 2" square from the middle by using a punch or a metal straightedge ruler and craft knife. Mat frame, if desired. Crop a piece of a page protector for the "glass" in the frame and mount to the back of the frame. Trim featured photo to size; center and mount behind frame with self-adhesive foam spacers for depth. "Hang" your photo from wire and a brad fastener when mounting on page. Close-up photos of objects and landscapes work well for frames or try this technique with enlarged photos, using a duplicate copy for the frame.

Mat color photos with black-and-white enlargement

When you look at this layout by Diana Hudson (Bakersfield, California), you get the feeling she matted her pictures with a beautifully painted canvas background—which is actually a black-and-white photo printed on canvas paper (Fredrix). A simple variation to this technique is to print a color enlargement on canvas paper for mat and mount black-and-white photos on it. Photos Mona Payne (Henderson, Nevada)

California

dreamin'

Joshua and Jordan really look forward to their annual summer vacation in Laguna Beach. After spending all day in the water, they like to walk around town in the evenings to visit their favorite shops and restaurants. The trip is not complete until they get ice cream and make a trip to the candy store. They think of Laguna as their second home.

You LIGHT UP the game!

When Jeffrey plays baseball, he is always a bright spot in the game. No matter what position he plays, he stands out and gives it his all for the team.   York County, VA   Oct 2002

Spotlight with a black-and-white background

When Ruthann Grabowski (Yorktown, Virginia) watches her son Jeffrey play baseball, he is all she sees during the game. To express this in her layout, Ruthann features a color photo segment atop a black-and-white duplicate photo to make him the focal point. Begin by making a black-and-white copy of a color photo. Use a metal straightedge ruler and craft knife to cut the desired focal subject from a square segment of the color photo; mat with cardstock. Mount the color image directly on top of the black-and-white copy in its original position. This technique is a great way to focus attention on a single person, or a small group of people in a crowd. For variation, use a black-and-white photo segment atop a color photo background and experiment with placing photo subject off-center.

wave chaser

Joshua

Laguna Beach

The boys love being on their boards so much that they will endure the often chilly Pacific Ocean for hours.

Mat a framed photo overlay on a photo background

Diana Hudson (Bakersfield, California) takes a playful photo and turns it into a charming layout by slicing and matting her main photo to a similar-themed photo, then mounting that to an enlarged version of the original. Use a window pattern cut from cardstock to help crop the frame overlay following the steps below. Photo Mona Payne (Henderson, Nevada)

1 Cut one 2¾" square from cardstock to form a window pattern. Cut one 3¼" square from cardstock to form window pattern. Discard resulting cardstock squares. Place smallest window pattern atop photo, center photo subject and trace lines of square on photo with a wax pencil. Repeat this step using the larger square, center over previously drawn small square, resulting in a set of square cutting lines that will form a frame on the photo.

2 Use a metal straightedge ruler and a craft knife to slice on cutting lines; remove resulting interior square frame and discard. Use a piercing awl or sewing needle to pierce holes in both frame and photo at all four interior corners. Thread fiber from back of photos, add a bead and tie in a knot on top of photo. Repeat for three remaining corners. To finish, mount new photo art atop background photo of similar subject for dimension.

Embellish a punched photo mat

Using an enlarged photo to serve as a mat for smaller photos gives any layout "eye appeal." But to take it to the next level, embellishing the mat is the way to go! Kelly Angard (Highlands Ranch, Colorado) does just that by adding baseball charms to go with her baseball photo layout. This would be a great idea to do with a larger event photo for a mat— and smaller snapshots of loved ones or friends at the event—with charms, punched shapes or beads to dangle as accents. Follow the steps below to create your own embellished photo mat.

1 Punch squares of desired size from cardstock. Arrange squares on back of photo, turning squares so they are in a diamond shape in desired position and leaving enough room between diamonds for setting an eyelet. Trace around diamonds with pencil. Use a craft knife and metal straightedge ruler to crop diamonds into photos to form windows.

2 Punch ⅛" holes between the diamond windows, insert the tubular end of an eyelet—one at a time—into each hole. Flip photo over. Insert eyelet setter into eyelet opening and tap firmly with a hammer until eyelet is almost flat. Remove setter, cover the eyelet with a soft cloth and tap hammer again to "finish" the set of each eyelet.

3 Cut a 1" length of wire. String wire through charm and through eyelet, wrapping wire around itself to "tie off." Use nylon jaw pliers to help flatten a bit, if desired. Cut excess wire with cutters. Repeat until all punched windows are accented with dangling charms.

Frame a color photo with a black-and-white photo

Trudy Sigurdson (Victoria, British Columbia, Canada) adds depth to her picture by cropping a frame out of a black-and-white copy. Start with a same-sized, black-and-white duplicate of a color photo. Use a ruler and a photo-safe wax pencil to mark the frame outline on the black-and-white photo. Secure the photo to cutting mat with removable artist's tape and crop out the center marked area with a metal straightedge ruler and craft knife. Double mat the color photo. Mount the black-and-white frame with self-adhesive foam spacers atop the color photo. You may also cut a piece out of a page protector to sandwich between the frame opening and matted photo for a faux glass look.

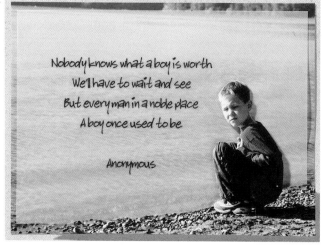

Frame a partial silhouette against a photo background

By using the partial silhouetting technique and a vellum piece over a photo background, Trudy Sigurdson (Victoria, British Columbia, Canada) makes her son look three-dimensional! Begin with two duplicate photos; the color and size of your reprints is not as important as having a photo subject that falls along one of the photo's edges. Using small, sharp scissors or a craft knife, partially silhouette crop the subject from one photo, leaving some of the foreground intact to become part of the frame. Print title or journaling on vellum; trim vellum into rectangle that is ⅛" smaller than photo size. Adhere vellum atop second photo and mat photo. Adhere partial silhouette atop vellum-laden photo, in its proper position in original image, with self-adhesive foam spacers for lift. For additional depth and variation, mount a frame cut from an additional copy of your photo atop the completed piece with foam tape doubled in thickness. This technique can be used whenever you desire to make a subject look as if it is coming right out of the photo.

Create a shadowbox photo frame

Shadowbox frames are an attractive way to display several different items all in one spot. The shadowbox concept is a natural for cropping photos creatively, as shown by MaryJo Regier's (Memory Makers) photo art. As you can see, a shadowbox photo frame gives you the ability to display several smaller pictures behind a sectioned photo frame. To make your own shadowbox photo frame, follow the instructions below. Complete the new photo art by adhering smaller, trimmed photos behind frame, centering photo subjects in cut squares. For variation, experiment with the placement of your square "windows" on the enlargement, or introduce sepia-toned or black-and-white photos into the project. You may also cut a piece out of a page protector to sandwich between the frame openings and smaller photos for a faux glass look.

1 Trace same-sized template squares atop photo enlargement using a photo-safe wax pencil, leaving equal distance between all squares. Use a craft knife and metal straightedge ruler to cut out squares.

2 Place photo on top of an 8 x 10" sheet of ⅛" thick foam core board, holding photo in place with a temporary adhesive. Trace photo windows onto foam core with a pencil.

3 Use a craft knife and metal straight-edge ruler to cut windows into foam core, cutting ⅛" outside of the traced lines so that foam core edges won't show through photo windows. Mount and adhere cropped enlargement to foam core with permanent adhesive.

Combine shadowboxes with partial silhouetting

Monique McCloskey (Oceanside, California) took her son Dylan to celebrate his birthday at California's LegoLand and not only came home with souvenirs but also some great photo memories. To incorporate the souvenirs into photo art, Monique used a layout with foam core for the shadow box. For special effect, a partial silhouette of the family helps draw the eye across the photo, into its recesses, and back to the family again. Although it may look like there are two copies of this photo, it is really just one. First, crop two segments from one enlarged photo as shown below to create the recesses in which to place mementos.

1 Use a photo-safe wax pencil and a graphing ruler to trace squares in the desired sizes based on the position of the photo subject you wish to crop into a partial silhouette. Use a craft knife and metal straightedge ruler to cut on straight lines. Use small, sharp scissors to crop around the photo subjects in a partial silhouette, leaving the outer edges of the bodies attached to the uncut photo. Wipe off any pencil residue from photo segments.

2 Place cropped photo on foam core board and trace squares, including shape of partial silhouette, onto foam core. Set photo aside. Use a craft knife and metal straightedge ruler to cut outside of traced lines. Use scissors to crop outside lines of partial silhouette. Cropping outside of traced lines ensures the foam core board won't show in finished art.

3 To assemble photo art, mount photo on top of foam core in its proper position, mat with black cardstock. Mount and adhere photo segments in the cut out recesses. Mount and adhere mementos as desired.

Crop a photo shaker box frame

Shaker boxes have become a very big thing in the scrapbooking world. To put a fresh twist on the trend, Kelly Angard (Highlands Ranch, Colorado) uses a photo as the top frame of her shaker box. Begin with two same-sized, subject-related photos—one for the frame and one for the background. To make a photo shaker box, follow the instructions below. Try this technique with birthday, baby, wedding, heritage, travel or holiday photos and add themed confetti, charms, punched shapes, beads or buttons in the shaker. Photos Chrissie Tepe (Lancaster, California)

1 Use a craft knife and metal straightedge ruler to cut a 1" frame from the top photo; discard resulting photo rectangle.

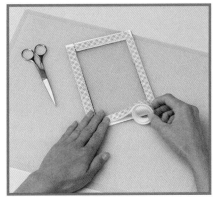

2 Cut a page protector ¼" larger than frame opening for "windowpane." Mount windowpane on back of photo frame. Cover outer edges of frame back with double-sided foam tape, making sure all edges are sealed completely.

3 Sprinkle some shells (U.S. Shell, Inc.) atop windowpane. Remove the foam tape backing; discard. Place and center background photo atop exposed foam tape to create shaker box.

Tole a photo silhouette

To give these pictures a 3-D effect, Jodi Amidei (Memory Makers) used silhouette-cropped flowers from duplicates of the original photo and an embossing stylus to curl the flowers just enough to give them the look she was after. Start with three duplicates of the same photo. Use small, sharp scissors to silhouette crop the flowers from first photo; save the scraps for title letters. Crop out the center of the flowers from the second photo. Follow the steps below to "tole" the flowers and flower centers. Mount flowers, then their centers, in their original positions on the third photo with self-adhesive foam spacers for lift. Try this with any curved photo subject to add dimension. Photo Sandra Yanisko (Barto, Pennsylvania)

1 Place silhouette-cropped photo pieces face down on a mouse pad. Rub an embossing stylus or the round tip of a bone folder around outer edges using a circular motion to curl. Rub lightly around entire photo. Repeat on all photo pieces to achieve tole effect.

Template-cut a self-framing photo

When Kelly Angard (Highlands Ranch, Colorado) looked at this adorable picture of her daughter, she was distracted by some of the background. Her solution? Kelly used a template and a craft knife to cut out the distractions while successfully framing the photo with itself. Follow the instructions shown to apply this technique to your photos. It's a super technique for all those pictures that you don't use because of the distracting backgrounds!

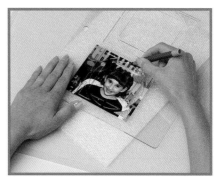

1 Place template (EZ2Cut Shapemakers by EZ2Cut/Accu-Cut) on photo and plastic foam cutting mat. Hold photo and template down with removable artist's tape, if desired. Insert a swivel blade knife into cutting channels to slice template pattern into photo. Discard resulting scraps.

Pierce an ornate, self-framing photo

To add more beauty to this happy picture, Jodi Amidei (Memory Makers) used a brass stencil to pierce a pretty pattern into a self-framing photo. Follow the illustration shown to create a self-framing photo using a brass stencil (Ornare™ by Ecstasy Crafts). Try varying the holes to make your own design. Make the holes slightly bigger and mount on contrasting paper for diversity. Photo Pam Klassen (Reedley, California)

1 Secure photo face up, centering focal point, to back of brass stencil with temporary adhesive. Cut slots from photo with a craft knife and discard. Place photo and stencil atop piercing mat or mouse pad. Use a piercing awl or sewing needle to pierce holes into photo following the design provided by the holes on the stencil.

1 Secure photo face up to back of brass stencil with temporary adhesive. Use a craft knife to carefully cut out stencil's pattern on photo. Set aside resulting frame. Place remaining photo center on plastic foam cutting mat and top with oval graduated template and center image. Use swivel blade knife to crop photo into an oval shape. Reassemble center in frame on cardstock.

Shadow-cut a self-framing photo

Shadow cutting a frame is an excellent way to draw your eye right into the focus of the photo while adding some interest to the framing effect itself. Jodi Amidei (Memory Makers) uses a brass "shadowing" stencil to create the butterfly pattern, and an oval graduated template (Coluzzle® by Provo Craft) to crop out the center. Follow the step at right to apply this technique to your photo. For variation, mat photo pieces with vellum, mulberry or textured paper. Photo Chrissie Tepe (Lancaster, California)

tearing

Once thought to be taboo in the world of scrapbooking, tearing photos is now enjoying popularity. Tearing can add drama or a soft and subtle look to photos, depending on the look you're trying to achieve. Removing the clear plastic backing from a photo can make tearing easier. Tear slowly to stay in control of the tear's direction.

Tear photos for a dramatic effect

MaryJo Regier (Memory Makers) gives an enticing picture a dramatic twist by tearing around the outer edges and matting it on black cardstock. Lay your picture face up for the tear to show rough, white edges (face down for tear to show smooth, clean edges). Place your left hand on the picture using your index finger as a guide for the tear. Use your right hand to tear around all of the edges of the photo, turning the photo as you go. Mat on black cardstock to emphasize torn edges.

Tear a unifying line across multiple photos

Making a unified tear across the top line of a photo series draws your eye right across the page and the story told in the photos. It also allows you to use more pictures on a single page layout as shown here by MaryJo Regier (Memory Makers). For a 12 x 12" layout, select five pictures from the same event. Trim the four that will go on the bottom of the page to 3" wide. For an 8½ x 11" layout, select four photos and cut three for the bottom 2¾" wide. Lay photos face down in reverse order; tape them all together making sure that you do not run tape along the "tearing edge." Turn taped photos right side up and tear the top edge toward you all the way across the top edges. Tear the top from the fifth photo also. Try using this technique with any photo sequence, such as sports photos, a toddler getting dressed, a baby rolling or a birthday party.

Soften torn edges

Torn photo edges lend an easygoing feel to scrapbook pages, but you can soften a torn edge even more with chalk. Kelly Angard (Highlands Ranch, Colorado) turned vivid color photos of her children into tender mementos of a sibling relationship by simply rubbing chalk onto the torn edges of the photos. First, tear photo edges—tearing pictures with the photo lying face up so that you will get the rough white edge on which to chalk. Then use your fingertip, a cotton swab or a sponge-tip makeup applicator to apply complementary-colored chalk on photo edges. To make the color deeper, add more chalk; to make the color softer, use less.

Burnt and faux-burnt torn edges

It has always been a favorite—dressing up and taking "old time" pictures. Adding a burnt edge to Kelly Angard's (Highlands Ranch, Colorado) picture of her son, gives it the conceptual feeling of it really being an old picture! There are two ways to do this technique. The first way is to use matches (above left). Tear photo edges leaving "burning room." Light a match and hold it to the edge of the picture. Blow it out when desired burnt look is achieved. Repeat this in small increments until all of photo and mat (if desired) are complete.

To create the look without the matches (which is safer in a scrapbook), brush tan, black and gray chalk onto the torn edges of the picture and mat (above right). For the final touch, use a fine-tip black marker to draw all along the edge of the tear.

Offset assemble a torn photo

Jodi Amidei (Memory Makers) proves that you can play a trick on the eye by taking a photo, tearing it and reassembling it offset for an effect deserving of a second look. Hold down a photo with your left hand using your index finger for your tearing guide. Tear toward you until it is torn all the way through the photo. Then tear the other side in the same way so that you have two larger end segments and one small center segment. Reassemble and mount offset so that the middle segment is higher or lower than the side segments, with each segment overlapping each other ever so slightly. Photo Torrey Miller (Thornton, Colorado)

Unite photos with diagonal tears

When you think football, you think rough and tough! MaryJo Regier (Memory Makers) does a fantastic job of giving you that feeling with the diagonal tears on the photos of her coach husband and ball-playing son. The photos—shot on different rolls of film on different days—stand united by the mirrored, diagonal tears. Tear photos toward you diagonally into three sections. Reassemble on page, leaving slight gaps in between the segments. Note how the direction of the torn lines leads the eye across the first photo and onto the second photo without missing a beat. Try it. A few well-placed tears can put the viewer's eyes right where you want them!

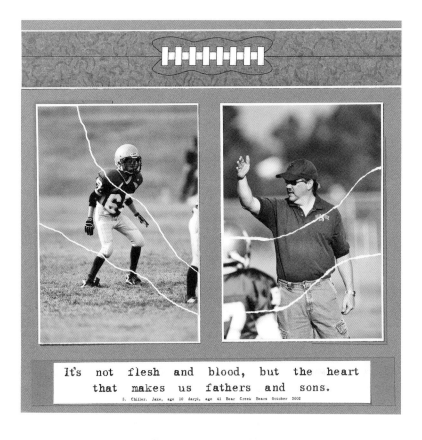

It's not flesh and blood, but the heart that makes us fathers and sons.

S. Chiller. Jake, age 10 daryl, age 41 Bear Creek Bears October 2002

Layer a torn photo

Diana Hudson (Bakersfield, California) takes a photo that, in its original form, may have had the focal point lost in all of the water in the background. By layering a torn copy with chalked edges, she adds interest while keeping the focus on the boy. Start with two copies of the same photo. Cut the first photo down to a more manageable size to handle when tearing. Tear around the focal point, making sure to tear toward you to get the rough edge. Chalk the torn edges lightly. Use self-adhesive foam spacers to mount the torn piece on the second photo, lining up the image in its proper position in the original photo. This technique is useful whenever you are looking for a way to bring the focal point to the forefront of the photo. Photo Mona Payne (Henderson, Nevada)

Tear a peek-a-boo window

MaryJo Regier (Memory Makers) captures a very sweet moment in black-and-white and frames it with a bold-colored peek-a-boo frame. The frame was a junk photo from the beginning of a roll of film that otherwise would have been tossed out. To make the frame, layer the two pictures together and place on a light box. If you do not have a light box, a brightly lit window will do. Mark four tearing points on the top photo with a photo safe wax pencil. Place the top photo onto a cutting mat and use a craft knife to start a cut large enough to get your fingers into to begin tearing the frame opening. Remember to leave some room for tearing. Start at one end of the cut and move around the entire shape tearing toward you. Mount the frame atop the peek-a-boo photo.

Tear a frame from an enlarged photo

Kelly Angard (Highlands Ranch, Colorado) uses an enlarged, snowy photo to make a frame for the photo of these sled dogs. She tears and rolls the opening of the frame to make it look as if it was torn back just to expose the sled dogs. To apply this technique, start with an 8 x 10" photo enlargement for the frame. Measure the peek-a-boo photo for an approximate opening size for the frame. Place enlarged photo on a cutting mat and cut out a general shape for the frame leaving enough room to then tear the opening. Tear around the cut-out shape and roll the torn edges back slightly with your fingers. Mount the second photo underneath the frame opening. For variation, try this technique with an old black-and-white copy underneath and burn the torn and rolled edges (see page 46).

Create a torn photo series montage

Expect the unexpected when you combine straight-cropped photos with randomly torn photos into a new photomontage. MaryJo Regier (Memory Makers) uses a photo series—one horizontal and three vertical shots—to capture a rugged, yet tender moment between father and son. Begin with one horizontal photo for the background. Use a craft knife and metal straight-edge ruler to cut the photo's subject into a square; mat with black paper and adhere back on photo. Tear three vertical photos into strips. Reassemble onto background photo to create the photomontage, lining up and matching photo subjects while tucking torn edges behind cropped and matted photo at center. For this type of photo art, shoot with camera from the same spot, pivoting left to right and overlapping some shots to capture movement in the scene. Turn camera horizontal and then vertical to get both types of shots, with elbows at the same height against your body (or use a tripod) while shooting to keep the subjects the same proportion with each progressive shot. A great technique for any photo series!

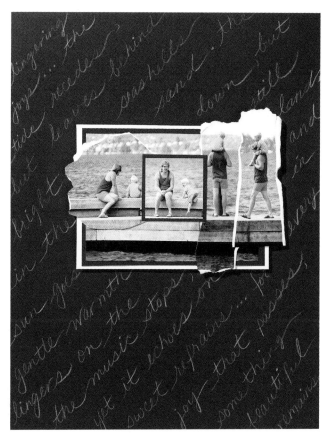

Tear photos to contrast positive and negative space

Brandi Ginn (Lafayette, Colorado) wanted to do a layout that showcased how much her family loves the snow. Cutting a heart shape from cardstock first for a pattern ensures a perfect torn photo heart. To create a torn heart and heart-shaped frames, see the step below. For a variation, try putting a picture underneath the torn heart frames or hang charms from the cutouts (see page 37).

1 Freehand cut a heart from cardstock. Use a photo-safe wax pencil to trace the heart pattern onto the photo. Make a small slit on the photo to begin a tear. Tear around drawn heart. Remove any pencil residue with a dry, soft cloth.

"All I need is my brains, my eyes and my personality, for better or for worse."

–William Albert Allard

shape cropping

Now that you have learned all about the basic, linear cropping of photos, shape cropping is a natural progression. With the wide array of theme-shaped templates and punches available, you may have a hard time deciding which ones to use to bring visual contour to your photographs! Here, you will discover how to:

- Crop photos into tags
- Frame a tag shaker box
- Slice shape pull-aparts
- Layer nested template shapes
- "Art deco" a panoramic photo series
- Switch shapes for positive/negative effect
- Use photos to create page titles
- Wrap lettering around a photo
- Crop reflected lettering
- Cut symbols into photos
- Lift randomly punched squares
- Punch and layer several photos
- Punch a thematic vignette or funky border
- Punch and slice interlocking photo tiles
- Combine circles and squares for a fold-out gallery
- Curl punched shapes for lift
- Punch a delicate or artsy edge
- Dangle a photo embellishment
- Stitch a suspended photo border

These well-defined cropping techniques will lend curvaceous structure and distinctive form to your photos and page layouts. In no time at all, you'll feel at ease and more than prepared to conquer cutting edge photo cropping techniques.

tags

There are limitless possibilities for incorporating photos into tag designs, which greatly increases the versatility of these much-loved page accents. Whether tags are freehand cut or cropped using a template, pattern or punch, one thing's for certain: These little photo accents have a huge impact!

Slice vertical strips

Jodi Amidei (Memory Makers) vertically slices a photo to feature her daughter's face and fade out the photo's background. See page 122 for tag pattern which can be used to create any of the tags on this spread. Mount pieces on tag leaving space between each slice. Slice a large or small photo either in equal or random segments depending on the tone and theme of your photo.

Punch a simple design

Add understated elegance to a photo tag with a punched design that doesn't overpower the photo. MaryJo Regier (Memory Makers) uses a punch (Missing Links Paper Shaper by EK Success) to punch a simple design. Use a decorative punch around the border of a photo or just at the corners for a delicate design.

Punch a vellum window

Trudy Sigurdson (Victoria, British Columbia, Canada) crops a window into a vellum overlay to highlight her daughter's face. Crop a photo into a tag shape either with a template or cutting system (Accu-Cut). Cut a piece of vellum into the same shape. Lay vellum over photo tag to determine where to cut or punch the "window." Cut out window; mount vellum over photo tag before adding embellishments and journaling. For extra interest, punch a single large window or a number of smaller windows to highlight various areas of a photo.

Layer a torn photo tag

A torn photo, layered with vellum on a tag, creates the perfect space for Trudy Sigurdson's (Victoria, British Columbia, Canada) thematic title. Cut two photos and one piece of vellum into a tag shape. Mount vellum on one photo tag. Diagonally tear a strip from second photo tag; mount over vellum, leaving space between the pieces as shown.

Frame a tag shaker box

Diana Hudson, (Bakersfield, California) makes use of two photos on a cleverly crafted tag shaker box. Use a template or die-cut system to cut two photos and a piece of foam core board into a tag shape. Follow the steps below to create a shaker box photo tag. Try this technique with any photo theme, including wedding, baby, school, travel and more. Finish tag by tying fibers, raffia or ribbon into hole and mount on page.

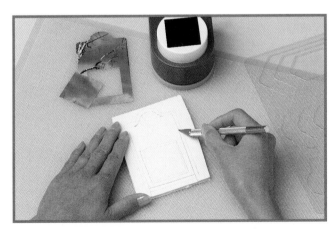

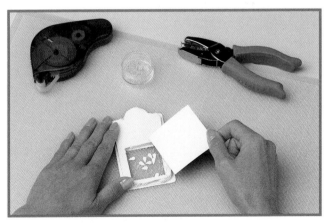

1 Cut tag shape into the photo using a tag template (Coluzzle® by Provo Craft) to form the front of the shaker box. Punch square (Emagination Crafts) in center of photo along lower edge to form "window." Trace tag template onto foam core board and cut out slightly inside traced marks with a craft knife to form shaker backing. Cut the foam core square portion slightly larger than the square window. Cut a square ¼" larger than window opening from a page protector to form shaker "glass." Center and adhere over picture tag with tape.

2 Adhere foam core piece to back of photo tag, placing adhesive around all sides of the window. Sprinkle beads and punched teardrops (Fiskars) atop window. Mount precut square background photo on back of window, adhering all sides completely to prevent beads and punched shapes from spilling out.

template shapes

The myriad of template shapes and types available provide a myriad of photo-cropping possibilities. Experiment with theme-shaped, geometric-shaped, graduated or nested, or panoramic-sized templates for stunning results that'll get more use out of your templates than ever before.

Slice a vertical background design

Jodi Amidei (Memory Makers) elaborates on a photo's theme with a vertically sliced palm tree with the help of a shape template. Trace shape with template on photo background. Cut apart with a continuous scissor stroke. Mount pieces, leaving space between each shape as shown. Photo Bruce Aldridge (Broomfield, Colorado)

1 Position template (Stamping Station) shape atop photo and trace shape with a wax pencil. If template shape is not long enough to reach from upper and lower edges of photo, draw two parallel lines about ¼" apart, connecting the drawn shape and forming continuous cutting lines.

2 Use small, sharp scissors to cut along drawn lines, making sure to use one continuous stroke of the scissors for a clean cut. Similar to silhouette cropping, have patience and move the photo in and out of the scissor blades instead of moving the blades around the shape.

3 Place the cut-apart photo slices in order on cardstock of choice, making sure to pull segments apart to allow background paper to show through. Adhere segments in place.

Slice a pull-apart design

Kelly Angard (Highlands Ranch, Colorado) horizontally slices stars and stripes into a large photo to reflect its patriotic theme. Trace a shape template onto a photo enlargement in desired positions with a wax pencil. Draw two horizontal lines about ¼" apart connecting the drawn shapes and forming continuous cutting lines. Cut along drawn lines using one continuous scissor stroke for a clean cut. Mount the cut-apart segments to background leaving a generous amount of space between pieces. Offset the cropped shape over segments with self-adhesive foam spacers for dimension as shown. Change the template shape to coordinate with your page and photo themes as desired. Photos JoAnn Petersen (Parker, Colorado)

Garden Girl

Step into my garden
Step in and you'll see
a measure of peace
and tranquility.

It's the scent of the blossoms
the buzz of the bees
the sweet song of birds
as they sing in the trees.

The sweet scent of roses
their petals so new
as they glisten and sparkle
with the fresh morning dew.

Run your toes through the grass
beneath a canopy of trees
hear the rustle of leaves
as they blow in the breeze.

Let the beauty of springtime
Fill your soul with great peace
Take it with you and share it
with each one you meet.

Create a kaleidoscope of color

Brandi Ginn (Lafayette, Colorado) adds a kaleidoscope of colors and shapes to her page with layers of floral photos cut from "nested templates." Follow the steps below to create layered photo page accents. Experiment with different photo themes, paper colors and layered shapes for varied results. Photos Michele Gerbrandt (Memory Makers)

1 Use a wax pencil to trace different nested template (Hot Off The Press) shapes atop photo duplicates. Use small, sharp scissors to cut out different shapes.

2 Mat cropped photo shapes with complementary-colored cardstock and reassemble to re-create original photo, using self-adhesive foam spacers between photo layers for dimension.

Layer nested template shapes

Kelly Angard (Highlands Ranch, Colorado) layers colorful sunset photos in designs cut from a nested template to achieve an elegant and dimensional embellishment. Trace template shapes onto different photos with the same theme. Mat each cropped photo on complementary-colored paper and silhouette around shape. Layer atop another with self-adhesive foam spacers for dimension.

Alternate black-and-white with color photo layers

Add visual appeal to a nested template design with black-and-white photos interspersed with color photo layers. Kelly Angard (Highlands Ranch, Colorado) achieves this look with two black-and-white and two color copies of the same photo. Trace nested template shapes onto photos, alternating color and black-and-white layers. Remount cropped shapes atop original image. Photo Erica Pierovich (Longmont, Colorado)

we left our hearts in san francisco, summer 2002

Slice a deco design in a panoramic photo

MaryJo Regier (Memory Makers) adds an interesting perspective to a panoramic skyline photo with a sliced and reassembled deco design. Follow the steps below to apply this technique to a panoramic photo. Experiment with this fun techniques using different photo themes and by varying the segments that you give dimension to with self-adhesive foam spacers.

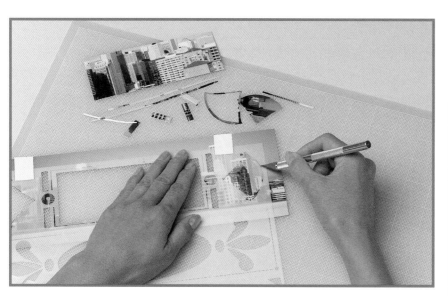

1 Place template (Scrapbook Magic) atop panoramic photo; hold both in place on cutting mat with removable artist's tape. Use a craft knife to cut out the template's different sections; set resulting photo pieces aside.

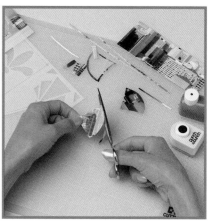

2 Use extended reach punches, if needed, to cut out the template's small circles, ovals or triangles. Trim ⅛" from outer edges of larger photo pieces using small, sharp scissors. Reassemble photo, mounting various photo shapes with self-adhesive foams spacers for dimension.

Swap color and black-and-white punched shapes

Jodi Amidei (Memory Makers) adds visual variation to a sliced and reassembled color and black-and-white photo with the swapping of punched shapes. Begin with a color and black-and-white copy of the same photo. Follow the steps below to create the photo art. After cropping, use all of the leftover photo triangles and punched circles to create a second piece of photo art for a gift! This simple technique works well for any photo theme.

Kent

You've taught me many things in life,
• how to speak my mind
• when I roam, I can still come back home
• there is no stronger bond than to love someone
• you're never too old to be a child
• wisdom comes from trial and error
• family ties may stretch but they never break

1 Layer color photo atop black-and-white photo and tape together with removable artist's tape. Use a metal straightedge ruler and craft knife to cut diagonally across the photos.

2 With photos still taped together, trace various template circles randomly onto photo triangles with a photo-safe wax pencil. Use a craft knife to carefully crop circles from layered photos. Or, use various-sized circle punches instead.

3 Separate layered photos. Reassemble large photo using one color and one black-and-white triangle. Adhere color circles in their original spot atop black-and-white photo. Adhere black-and-white circles in their original spot atop color photo.

letters

It's quick and easy to incorporate letters into your photo art. Whether you're cropping letters directly into your photos, revealing the negative space left behind by cropped letters or cropping letters from photo scraps, photo lettering provides custom-coordinated page accents.

Watch for opportunities within a photo

Sometimes a photo will unwittingly provide you with title letters that you can build upon as Jennifer Whitten (Stephenville, Texas) discovered with a poolside photo of her children. Round corners of photo. Cut P and L letters and arrange with photo to spell "pool." Experiment with posing people in photos in certain ways or with certain objects to help create lettering that could prove useful on a scrapbook page.

Crop photo into title letters

Build on the theme of your page and make a bold statement with photos cut into title letters. MaryJo Regier (Memory Makers) humorously incorporates photos of her sons' marble collection into a dimensional title that looks like it's ready to roll off the page. Use a template or die-cut system to cut letters from photos. This technique makes good use of photo scraps, extra photos or preprinted photo strips. Consider photographing the items being used in a photo to create title letters. Inspired by Angelia Wigginton (Belmont, Mississippi)

Minnesota:
Land of 10,000 Lakes
and not a single fish today...
But there's always lots of sand!

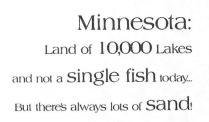

West Battle Lake

June 22, 1996

Jake (4) and Dylan (7)

Punch a title into a photo

A creative use of negative space is achieved with the help of letter punches. MaryJo Regier (Memory Makers) punches a vertical title into the background of a treasured photo of her son, saving space and personalizing the photo at the same time. Punch title letters horizontally or vertically in a photo depending upon background space available. Set punched photo letters aside or mount elsewhere on the page for an extra embellishment.

Reveal letters in negative photo space

Pamela Frye Hauer (Denver, Colorado) makes a bold statement with large letters carefully cut into a photomontage. Create this look by first composing a photomontage; adhere photos together and tack down on cutting mat with a temporary adhesive. Use a large lettering template or create your own letter pattern by printing letters from the computer. Place pattern over area to be cut out. Trace with wax pencil and carefully slice out shape with a craft knife, making sure to hold photos together when slicing. Mount photos onto contrasting colored cardstock to make letters stand out.

Slice numbers into photomontage

Terri Sharp (Hillsborough, New York) illustrates how fun it can be to incorporate sliced numbers into a photomontage to commemorate a Disney anniversary during her family's travels. Begin by assembling the photomontage and tack down on cutting mat with a temporary adhesive. Use large number templates or create your own numbers pattern by printing numbers from the computer. Place pattern over area to be cut out. Trace with wax pencil and carefully slice out shape with a craft knife, making sure to hold photos together when slicing. Mount photos onto contrasting colored cardstock to make numbers stand out.

Carve letters into photos

Holle Wiktorek (Clarksville, Tennessee) integrates part of her page's title with images on her page by "carving" the letters into a series of five photos. Crop a series of vertical photos to fit page, making sure each photo is wide enough for its intended letter. Use a template to trace the letter onto the photo with a wax pencil; select an area in the photo that doesn't interfere with its focal point. Using a craft knife, carefully carve the letter into the photo.

As terrorists strike and there is threat of war with the Middle East, I am reminded of good times in my life. Attending family gatherings, bowling on lazy afternoons, building snowmen, climbing on Daddy's shoulders, and decorating for Christmas...these are the things that matter. If terrorists would spend more time focused on family and happiness, they could enjoy the true power of peace. I wish they would take control of their own happiness instead of hurting others. If it could only be that easy...all I can do is pray.

We cruised in the Corvair for nine glorious summers. Wind in our hair, sun on our faces, and the AM radio blaring oldies made us feel young again. We knew we wanted a classic, something that could hold a couple car seats, and it had to be a convertible. But the lack of shoulder harnesses meant that we only took her on short trips down slow streets.

She reigned over the garage instead of the road. There was a woman in Ohio who had been having her own dreams of Corvair summers with open sky above. She made an offer and a trucking company picked up the car. We never regretted buying the Corvair, but we knew it was time to let go.

1966
Corvair
Corsa
Convertible

Highlight negative space of carved letters

A classic black-and-white photo provides the perfect backdrop for Kelli Noto's (Centennial, Colorado) steady hand and talent for using a craft knife. Create a pattern for title words by printing letters from the computer; silhouette cut. Place letters on top of photo and trace. Carefully cut out letters with a craft knife. Mount carved photo over monochromatic-colored cardstock to highlight words.

Crop and layer letters onto enlargement

This creatively cropped page requires three 8 x 10" prints of the same photograph and can be accomplished using just about any photo theme. First, mat one uncropped 8 x 10" photo with paper or cardstock. Create photo letters from additional 8 x 10" prints as described below. Art by Pam Klassen (Reedley, California); Based on a submission by Sharon Kropp of C-Thru Ruler Co. (Bloomfield, Connecticut); Photo Kris Perkins (Northglenn, Colorado)

1 Using a lettering template (Better Letter by C-Thru Ruler Co.), position a letter on an 8 x 10" print. Trace and cut out with a craft knife.

2 Repeat Step 1 for each letter, cutting the 1st and 3rd letters from one photo and the 2nd and 4th letters from the other. Use paper letters for positioning.

3 Mount each photo letter on cardstock. Use small, sharp scissors to cut around the mat edges. Leave about ⅛" margins.

4 Carefully layer each photo letter on the uncut 8 x 10" photo so that the images are aligned with the background photo.

Enhance carved letters with soft details

Letters carved out of an enlarged photo provide a window for Kathleen Childers' (Christiana, Tennessee) soft paper torn strip. Create this layered look by following the tips below. Try this with any photo subject—or better yet, make a deliberate effort to photograph objects in close-up that appear in your people shots.

1 Use a wax pencil and graphing ruler to measure and draw a vertical line down the center of photo and a horizontal line across the center of photo to help pinpoint the photo's exact center. Place lettering template (EZ2Cut Shapemakers by EZ2Cut/Accu-Cut) on photo and starting at the center of the photo, insert swivel craft knife into appropriate letter's channel and cut. Repeat step, working from center and going outward, until entire title is spelled out with even spacing between each letter.

Wrap photo letters around photos

Scenic title letters wrap around Kelly Angard's (Highlands Ranch, Colorado) camping photos, adding smaller creative and visual elements to the larger photos. Cut letters using a template and craft knife. Mount photo letters around photos in an eye-pleasing manner. Experiment with horizontal, vertical or diagonal placement for variation.

Assemble a reflective title

A reflective title cut from a collection of thematic photos makes for an interesting showcase of images. Kim Rudd (Idledale, Colorado) assembled her reflective title with photos that contained still water reflections, but any photos containing mirrored images or reproduced with a reverse image will work. Follow the tips below to create this look with your photos.

1 Trace letters with a wax pencil and use a craft knife and scissors to cut them out. To create reflected lettering, simply flip the template (Better Letter by C-Thru Ruler Co.) upside down on photo directly below original letter and trace and cut.

Watch for surname in photographed signs

A fun-filled trip to Disney Adventures theme park had Jeanne Ciolli (Dove Canyon, California) thinking in terms of the perfect scrapbook page. While at the theme park, she posed her family around the large letters of the entrance sign with creative thoughts brewing in her mind. Silhouette-crop photo letters and nestle amongst a colorfully collaged background for a unique title. Watch for your surname within the decorative lettering of signs while traveling for one-of-a-kind page titles!

Use leftover photos for illuminated letters

It's easy to incorporate photo scraps into page title lettering like Pam Klassen (Memory Makers) did for these custom-coordinated, illuminated looks. Simply crop or punch the photo scrap into a shape, then back or mat with cardstock or additional photo scraps. For variation, try mounting cardstock letters on top of the cropped photo scraps. Photos Debbie Mock (Memory Makers), Pamela Frye Hauer (Denver, Colorado), Sandra De St. Croix (St. Albert, Alberta, Canada), Lora Lee Dischner (Denver, Colorado)

symbols

Symbols offer a universal language all their own, and when cropped into photos, the message can be twice as effective. Use dies, templates, patterns or freehand to cut symbols into photos for token appeal!

Craft a photomontage symbol

Holle Wiktorek (Clarksville, Tennessee) found a clever way to announce the sex of her friends' unborn child by piecing together a photomontage into the international female symbol. To create your own photo symbol, follow the tips below. Use a light box or a keen eye to lay photos over the symbol one at a time, making sure the desired images won't be trimmed off. Be creative with other symbols that relate to the theme of your photos like a heart, international male symbol, cross or other religious symbol.

1 Enlarge and photocopy female symbol pattern on page 122. If desired, cut pattern into as many pieces as the number of photos you wish to include in the new photo art. Position pattern pieces over photos randomly to capture desired images; cut with scissors. Reassemble new art on cardstock background.

Slice a related symbol into a photo

A spiritual symbol freehand cut into a photo by Jodi Amidei (Memory Makers) enhances a drab background while maintaining religious reverence. Freehand draw (or use the pattern on page 122) of any related symbol onto a photo with a wax pencil before slicing with a craft knife. Wipe any remaining wax residue from photo surface with a soft cloth. Photo Brenda Martinez (Lakewood, Colorado)

Die cut a symbol

Jodi Amidei (Memory Makers) makes a bold statement of patriotic peace with an international symbol die cut into an enlarged photo. Use the photo die cut elsewhere on your page to reinforce its intended meaning without the use of words.

1 Place photo face up on foam side of die (Accu-Cut) and center die beneath area of photo where you wish to cut symbol. Place die foam side up on die tray; roll through machine (Accu-Cut) to cut the symbol's shape.

punches

Punch manufacturers continue to launch new punch shapes and styles, providing scrapbookers with a never-ending supply of photo-cropping tools. Give punches a try on your photos—it's a punch of fun!

Exaggerate elements in a photo series

Cropped segments of an enlarged photo are reassembled in MaryJo Regier's (Memory Makers) photo series, adding an exaggerated element to her athletic son. Reprint photos in a variety of sizes for an interesting way to highlight desired elements in a photo. Punch photo images into square, geometric or free-form shape and reassemble in a vertical or horizontal line. Try this with any photo where magnification of an element in the photo could be funny, such as that big fish catch or an eye-popping expression.

Add a delicate corner touch

Torrey Miller (Thornton, Colorado) softens a photo of delicate yet hardy pansies with a simple punched corner treatment. Use a small square punch to punch two diagonal squares from one photo corner. Mount the punched photo and photo square stair-stepped diagonally as shown. Experiment with this technique using different geometric-shaped punches on different photo corners or borders for variation. Photo Jodi Amidei (Memory Makers)

Add dimension to randomly punched squares

Trudy Sigurdson (Victoria, British Columbia, Canada) gives a portrait of her children a "lift" with randomly punched squares mounted back in place with self-adhesive foam spacers. Turn punch over and insert photo to capture desired image before punching. Mount punched photo squares back in place with self-adhesive foam spacers in a variety of thicknesses for dimensional interest.

Punch a duplicate photo

Trudy Sigurdson (Victoria, British Columbia, Canada) uses a different approach to the above technique but basically achieves the same effect. Punch details into a duplicate photo with square punches in a variety of sizes. Mount squares over original images with self-adhesive foam spacers. Reprint duplicate photos either in black-and-white, sepia or a colored tone for a contemporary graphic look.

Punch a scenic border

Pam Kuhn's (Bryan, Ohio) visual ensemble of Boston's cityscape is featured with punched "windows" and dimensional details. Stack three different cityscape photos for the background. Cut ½" off each end of a duplicate set; cut or punch window in the center of each photo before matting on one piece of patterned paper. Cut or punch a smaller square in the center of each matted photo; mount over background photos with self-adhesive foam spacers for dimension. Punch four other city scenes; mat and mount on top layer of stacked photos.

Punch a thematic vignette

Kelly Angard (Highlands Ranch, Colorado) used a square punch to focus in on elements of interest and showcase a number of photos in her thematic vignette. Punch square shapes into photos. Turn punch over and insert photo to capture desired image. Single and double mat photos; place around large photo of the same theme as shown. Try this with wedding, baby, school, travel and heritage photos for a unique photo essay.

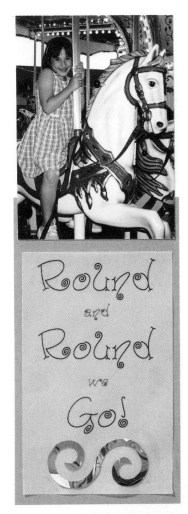

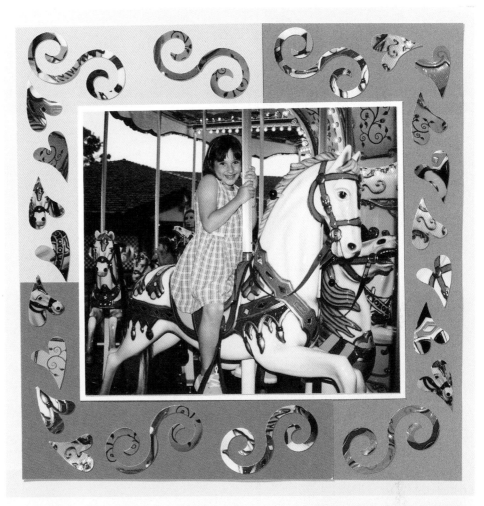

Create a frame with punched photo pieces

Decorative shapes, punched from duplicate photos, enhance Kelly Angard's (Highlands Ranch, Colorado) photo frame with a kaleidoscope of color. Turn punch shape over to capture desired images from photo background. Select shapes that work with the theme of your photos. Experiment with other punched shapes for variation.

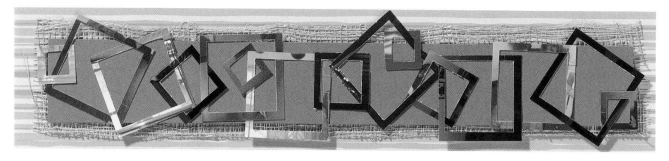

Punch a geometric photo border

Jill Tennyson's (Lafayette, Colorado) punched geometric border makes good use of leftover photo scraps. Square shapes, in a variety of sizes, are punched and then re-punched to achieve a thin photo frame. Slice through one edge of punched square frames to link shapes together. Mount linked shapes in an asymmetrical, eye-pleasing fashion.

Punch interlocking photo tiles

MaryJo Regier (Memory Makers) links together punched photo shapes representing the symbolic bond between sisters. Follow the instructions below to create the interlocking photo tiles. This is a great technique to use on photos of family or friends. If you use photos that all have different-colored backgrounds, the small half-diamonds that result from interlocking will be more prominent.

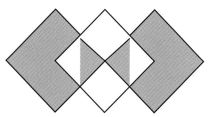

1 Punch a number of large square photo shapes. Turn on end to form a diamond; determine the sequence of order to link together. Or enlarge and photocopy the diamond photo tile patterns on page 122 to fit photo subject, noting that the cut lines on each pattern is different. Trace diamonds atop desired photos with a wax pencil; cut out to create photo tiles. Use a craft knife and a metal straightedge ruler to slice the photo tiles for locking them together. Interlock photo tiles as shown in the diagram above.

Fold out a gallery of punched photos

A collection of punched photos from a memorable vacation is neatly packaged in a mini fold-out album. Heidi Schueller's (Waukesha, Wisconsin) European photo gallery is made up of punched photos mounted on cardstock squares and linked together with ribbon. To create a fold-out photo gallery, cut twelve 3 x 3" squares of cardstock and ten 1" strips of ribbon for connectors. Apply double-sided adhesive to both sides of ribbons and sandwich ribbons between pairs of cardstock squares to form fold-out; mount fold-out on page. Use a jumbo circle punch to crop photos and journaling blocks; adhere to both sides of fold-out if desired.

Randomly punch positive/negative shapes

Julie Mullison (Superior, Colorado) builds on a bubbly theme with randomly punched circles placed along her photo's edge. Punch large circles first and work down to smallest punch for an overall balanced look. Flip punch over to ensure desired placement. Mount punched shapes just outside of negative punched space for an interesting effect.

Punch a contemporary edge

Kelly Angard (Highlands Ranch, Colorado) punches a little geometric fun into a futuristically themed photo, shaping a unique and eye-catching edge. Randomly punch circle shapes in a variety of sizes along the outside of a photo. Mount punched shapes along the edge to extend the photo's border as shown. This takes some time and patience, but the results are well worth it!

Punch a family tree

Documenting a family's birth line doesn't have to be a complicated project as demonstrated by Kim Rudd's (Idledale, Colorado) simple punched vignettes. Turn circle punch over to center faces before punching. Use a singular shape for consistency, or a different shape to differentiate matriarchal and patriarchal families.

Punch dimensional shape into a photo

Colorful punched poinsettias blossom from JoAnn Colledge's (North Ogden, Utah) photos with realistic dimension and sparkling details. Follow the instructions below to create photo blossoms. Detail flower centers with glitter glue. This technique works well to enhance and embellish a variety of related photos and punches.

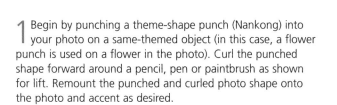

1 Begin by punching a theme-shape punch (Nankong) into your photo on a same-themed object (in this case, a flower punch is used on a flower in the photo). Curl the punched shape forward around a pencil, pen or paintbrush as shown for lift. Remount the punched and curled photo shape onto the photo and accent as desired.

Punch a delicate corner design

Decorative corner punches add a hint of color and design to the corners of Kelly Angard's (Highlands Ranch, Colorado) black-and-white portraits. Punch corners of cropped photo; layer on colored paper. Detail photo mat with designs punched from colored paper. You can also experiment with punching a decorative border across the top, bottom or sides of a photo by removing corner punch guides. Flip the punch over and insert photo edge; repeat as needed across the photo.

Punch a decorative edge

Torrey Miller (Thornton, Colorado) adds a unique edge to a photo with a decorative border punch. Line up the repetitive design using the guideline marks on the punch (Border Punch by Fiskars) or flip the punch over to ensure proper spacing of a continuous design. Photo Jodi Amidei (Memory Makers)

Flip a positive shape to reveal negative space

MaryJo Regier (Memory Makers) emphasizes the destructive force of nature with related shapes punched into her photos and achieves interesting positive/negative effects at the same time. Flip over rectangle and fern punches (Family Treasures, Martha Stewart respectively) to capture desired image; mount punched shape upside down, giving a reflective look to the finished artwork.

Embellish and dangle punched photo shapes

Punched leaves dangle in the negative space of a large punched shape as a decorative background element on MaryJo Regier's (Memory Makers) fall photo. Punch two mega birch leaves into the background of an enlarged photo. Repunch resulting mega birch leaves with a large birch punch. Attach eyelets to photo above punched negative space. Punch ¹⁄₁₆" hole in large birch leaves. Dangle large birch leaves from spiraled and beaded wire through eyelet. Secure wire to back of photo with artist's tape. Punch ¹⁄₁₆" holes in mega birch leaves. String together with a twist of beaded wire for an accent.

Punch a shadowbox border

Jodi Amidei (Memory Makers) adds sweet details to a portrait with a punched shadowbox border. Punch squares down the left side of a photo; flip punch over for even placement. Adhere foam tape to the back of the punched photo before matting for shadowbox effect. Punch small shapes from leftover photo scraps; mount in windows with self-adhesive foam spacers. Photo Bruce Aldridge (Broomfield, Colorado)

A dream is a path to the future
A quiet belief in the heart,
A small secret wish nurtured deep in a spirit
where all great accomplishments start.

A dream is an endless horizon
That only a dreamer can see.
A dream is a challenge...
A promise of all you can be.

Stitch together a suspended border

Kelly Angard's (Highlands Ranch, Colorado) punched and re-punched seaside photos are carefully stitched together to form a suspended photo border. Crop photos into squares. Flip large circle punch over and center square before punching. Re-punch resulting circles with sun, sailboat and clamshell punches (Emagination Crafts, Nankong), again turning the punches over to center each image. Mount punched and re-punched shapes on patterned paper square and mat on torn cardstock squares. Pierce holes with paper-piercing tool or sewing needle before stitching together with embroidery thread.

"You can't depend on your eyes if your imagination is out of focus."

–Mark Twain

artistic cropping

Now you are ready to unleash your basic and shape-cropping finesse on these simple yet artistic photo-cropping techniques. These crisp ideas will have you transforming your photos into uniquely clever art with little to no effort at all. Turn the pages to find ways to:

- Top a woven background with a silhouette-cropped photo

- Weave an interlocking heart

- Weave photo corners to form a frame

- Freehand cut a woven loom photo

- Weave photos with a graduated template

- Freehand cut a random mosaic

- Make a partial mosaic border

- Crop a silhouette-embedded mosaic

- Float a double-sided mosaic

- Crop a diamond mosaic

- Piece together a 3-D mosaic

- Cut and assemble abstract linear, circle, lifetime, quilt, shapely, mind-blowing and "handy" photo collages

- Create a breezy photo pinwheel

- Slice hinged doors and peek-a-boo panels

- Make bobblehead and animal cut-outs

- Crop movement into photos with wire, slide pulls and wheels

Artistic photo cropping techniques shine with the tasteful, aesthetic flair that will teach you how to become a photo-cropping virtuoso. You'll never look at your photos and scrapbook supplies quite the same again!

weaving

Photo weaving has gained immensely in popularity, and these fresh new twists on the art are sure to get you inspired to experiment. With a few slices here and a few weaves there, photos take on texture without added bulk.

Within the layout image:

Vancouver Island in B.C. is one of the most beautiful places to live and all along its coast are smaller islands with equally breathtaking views. One of my favorites is

Newcastle Island

Newcastle Island is a tiny island that is about a 10 minute ferry ride just off the coast of Nanaimo. Long ago, people actually lived on it as they were mining coal. That's hard to believe as now its only visitors are day trippers and campers who want to stay at it's campgrounds. When you step off the ferry, the first thing you see is this impressive totem pole that looks as if it's guarding the Island. My favorite part of the Island though, is the incredible sand stone beaches. They are like nothing I've ever seen before and it was on these beaches that I collected the sand dollars that are included on this layout. July 2002

Weave a photo background

A woven photo becomes a textured and mosaic-like background for Trudy Sigurdson's (Victoria, British Columbia, Canada) silhouette-cropped totem pole. Enhance the focal point of any photo using this technique by starting with three copies of the same photo. Refer to the step shots on the following page to create the photo art. This weaving technique will work well with any photo that has a fairly large subject at the center of the photo.

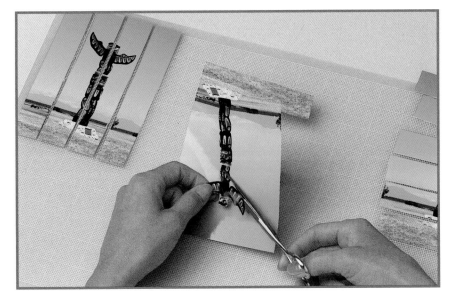

1 Use a craft knife and metal straight-edge ruler to slice the first duplicate photo into four 1" wide vertical strips. Slice the second duplicate photo into six 1" wide horizontal strips. If desired, letter or number the back of all photo strips to keep them in consecutive order for weaving. Use small, sharp scissors to silhouette crop subject from the third duplicate photo, being careful to stay true to the subject's outline and not lob off any necessary parts.

2 Weaving begins in the center, starting with two vertical photo strips and two horizontal strips. Weave all strips together, matching photo features to re-create original photo. Secure loose ends with adhesive.

3 Apply self-adhesive foam spacers, cutting as needed to fit, to back of silhouette-cropped photo. Mount in its proper position atop woven photo background.

Weave an interlocking heart

The blending of two lives is symbolically woven together into Jodi Amidei's (Memory Makers) interlocking photo heart. A black-and-white and sepia-toned photo are partially sliced into strips and then woven together to create a dual-toned image. Enlarge the pattern on page 122 and follow the step shots below to weave a shaped image. Photo Lydia Rueger (Memory Makers)

1 Start with a black-and-white and a sepia-toned duplicate of the same photo. Layer photos and hold together with temporary adhesive. Enlarge and photocopy the pattern on page 122 twice; cut patterns out. Join the two pattern pieces together to form a heart; tape together with a temporary adhesive. Position heart pattern atop layered photos; cut around outer edges with scissors. This will result in one black-and-white photo heart and one sepia-toned photo heart. Cutting at the same time is important so that the cuts are exact on both photos.

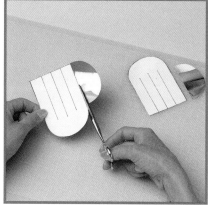

2 Place the second pattern piece atop the left side of the sepia-toned, heart-shaped photo; trim off remaining photo edge on right side. Place the pattern piece atop the right side of the black-and-white, heart-shaped photo; trim off remaining photo edge on left side. Use a craft knife and metal straightedge ruler to slice the three cutting lines on both photos.

3 Follow the diagram to weave the black-and-white and sepia-toned photo halves together, weaving over and under as you go. Secure loose ends with adhesive.

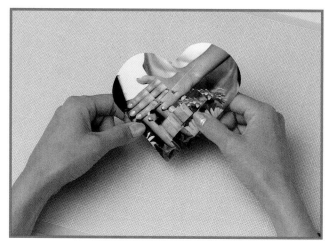

Weave a self-framing photo

Sliced photo strips woven at the corners become a complementary framing variation that doesn't detract from Valerie Barton's (Flowood, Mississippi) photo. Horizontally slice two ¼" strips from the top and two ¼" strips from the bottom of a duplicate photo. Slice two ¼" strips from the left and right sides of the original photo. Crop ½" off the top and bottom of the original photo; mount cropped photo at center of background cardstock. Mount horizontal strips above and below cropped photo, leaving a small amount of space between strips. Leave the ends of strips loose; adhere only the center of the strips. Weave vertical strips on left side of photo in an under/over fashion at ends, starting with the strip closest to the cropped photo. Repeat process with strips on the right side. Secure all ends with adhesive.

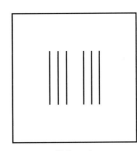

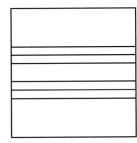

Pattern A   Pattern B

Weave photo strips into sliced slots

Sliced strips are woven into slots, framing the focal point of Brandi Ginn's (Lafayette, Colorado) floral photo. Refer to the step below to create the photo art. Try this framing technique with any photo that has the focal point at the photo's center.

1 Start with two copies of the same photo. Enlarge and photocopy woven panel patterns A & B on page 123. Trim photo to same size as patterns. Hold pattern A atop one photo with removable artist's tape; use craft knife and metal straightedge ruler to slice through the six cutting lines on pattern to form slots. Hold pattern B atop second photo with removable artist's tape; use a craft knife and metal straightedge ruler to slice through the photo on the cutting lines. Weave the four resulting thin slices into the photo frame slots lining up to match original image as shown; discard the remaining three thick slices.

Freehand cut a weaving loom

A freehand-cut loom, sliced into a color photo, provides a framework for weaving in black-and-white photo strips. Kelly Angard (Highlands Ranch, Colorado) integrates black-and-white photo strips into a duplicate color photo sliced into a loom using a traditional under- and over-weaving technique. Follow the step shots on the next page to weave a dramatic and contrasting work of art. Photos Erica Pierovich (Longmont, Colorado)

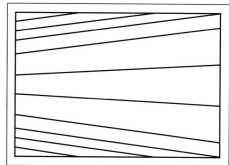

1 Enlarge and photocopy photo loom pattern on page 123 to fit a color 5 x 7" photo, either horizontal or vertical. Mount pattern on the back of your photo with temporary adhesive. Use a metal straightedge ruler and craft knife to slice through cutting lines as shown to create the "loom," being careful not to cut all the way through to photo's edges. Discard the used pattern.

2 For a horizontal color 5 x 7" photo, slice black-and-white photo into $\frac{1}{10}$" and $\frac{3}{10}$" strips alternately. Discard the smaller slices.

3 Weave the remaining larger slices back into the color photo, moving them into their proper position in the original image. Secure any loose ends with adhesive.

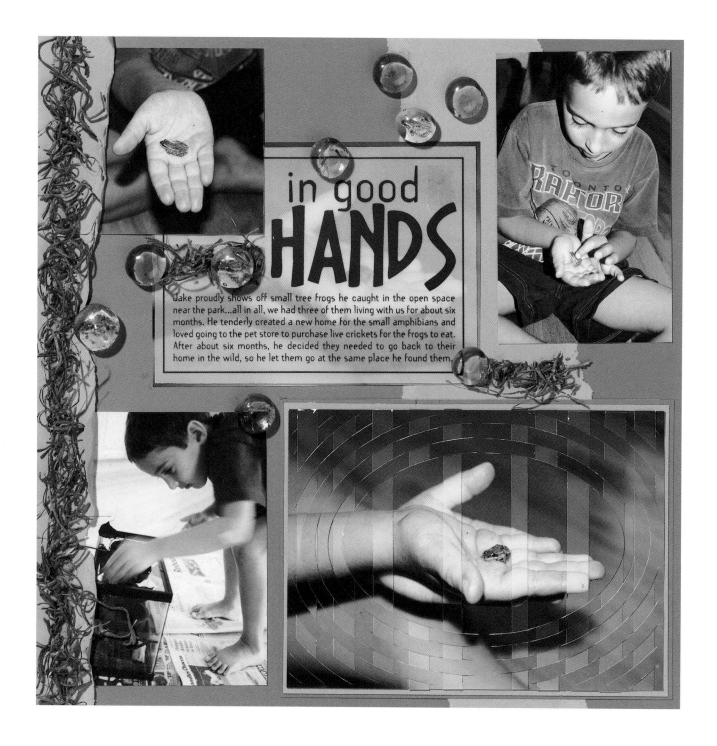

Jake proudly shows off small tree frogs he caught in the open space near the park...all in all, we had three of them living with us for about six months. He tenderly created a new home for the small amphibians and loved going to the pet store to purchase live crickets for the frogs to eat. After about six months, he decided they needed to go back to their home in the wild, so he let them go at the same place he found them.

Make a graduated template loom

An oval-cutting graduated template makes it easy to create an oval loom for photo weaving. Kelly Angard's (Highlands Ranch, Colorado) woven design gives a strong sense of focus when the photo subject is at the center of the design. Try other shapes of graduated templates to make a varied loom. To re-create this look, start with one 5 x 7" color photo and one 5 x 7" black-and-white duplicate. Create the photo loom by following the steps on the facing page.

1 Place the nested oval template (Coluzzle® by Provo Craft) over color photo on a plastic foam cutting mat. Insert the swivel knife into a template-cutting channel and make the cut. Repeat until all desired template channels are cut, being careful to stop the cuts before you reach the outer edges of the photo to keep the rings of the loom intact and connected to the cropped photo.

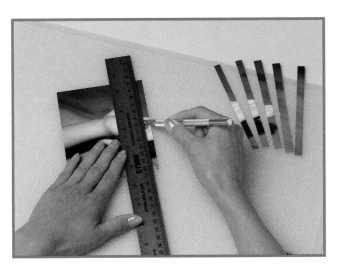

2 Use a metal straightedge ruler and craft knife to slice the black-and-white photo into ¼" and ⅜" vertical strips. Only nine strips will be woven back into the color photo loom; the rest will be discarded.

3 Weave select strips vertically into the oval loom, alternating between the two strip sizes as desired and lining up images in their original position in the color photo. Repeat as needed, pulling photo strips over and under the oval-cropped rings until a total of nine strips are woven back into the photo.

mosaics

Just when you thought you'd seen all of the techniques possible for photo mosaics, along comes a new generation of photo mosaic art. You'll fall in love with these fresh embedding, floating, diamond and three-dimensional "tiling" techniques.

Design a freehand-cut mosaic

Jodi Amidei (Memory Makers) fools the eye with two techniques that give a similar free-form mosaic effect. Graceful wavy lines are cut into the first photo (on the left) and reassembled, leaving space between each piece to form the mosaic. The same effect is achieved on the photo on the right, only instead of cutting the photo apart, Jodi scratched the surface emulsion into wavy lines with a piercing tool or sewing needle. Utilize the free-form element showing that the beauty of this type of mosaic is in the imperfections. Photo Kelli Noto (Centennial, Colorado)

Crop a mosaic border

Crop and reassemble segments of a photo into a partial mosaic border for an eclectic variation of mosaic photo art. Heather Parnau (Sussex, Wisconsin) cropped 1" squares from corners of one photo, and a succession of squares along the left side of another photo. Reassemble cropped squares and mount on matting with eyelets as shown here, or implement decorative brad fasteners for a little extra fun.

Crop a mini mosaic within a photo

A mini mosaic, cropped into Kathleen Fritz's (St. Charles, Missouri) photo provides eye-catching relief to a large background while it mimics the ship's netting design. Using a craft knife and metal straightedge ruler, slice a square out of an enlarged photo. Punch or cut small squares from photo square. Reassemble and mount leaving a small amount of space between each piece. Challenge your creativity by inserting a mini mosaic of another photo into the cut out negative space.

Surround silhouette-cut image with mosaic tiles

Valerie Barton's (Flowood, Mississippi) silhouette-cropped rose is lifted from a mosaic-cut background giving dimension to its blooming elements. Follow the step shots below to add artistic effects to a silhouette-cropped photo. Try this technique with any photos that have a focal point that can be easily silhouette-cropped and have an uncomplicated background conducive to cutting into mosaic tiles.

1 Silhouette crop photo subject from photo with a craft knife or small, sharp scissors—being careful not to cut through any of the edges of the photo; set aside. The idea is to remove a chunk of the center of the photo, leaving the photo edges intact.

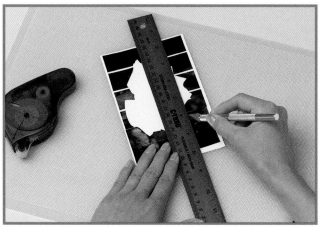

2 Tape the remainder of the photo to cutting mat with temporary adhesive. Use a craft knife and metal straightedge ruler to cut the remainder of the photo into 1" strips vertically, then repeat horizontally, resulting in 1" square photo tiles. Reassemble mosaic, adding silhouette-cropped photo at center.

Embed small photos into a large mosaic

Kelli Noto (Centennial, Colorado) intersperses small action images and details of the game into a large mosaic. Follow the step shots below to cut and reassemble a mosaic made of 1" squares. Use this mosaic technique with an enlarged photo that has a background conducive to replacing some of its tiles with small themed photos.

1 Make a grid pattern across the back of your photo with temporary adhesive to hold it firmly to cutting mat as you crop. Use a craft knife and metal straightedge ruler to cut vertical slices at 1" intervals down the length of the photo. Then cut horizontally across the vertical slices at 1" intervals to create mosaic photo tiles.

2 Reassemble large mosaic onto cardstock background of choice. Then strategically remove photo tiles "here and there" without disrupting too much of the original mosaic. Replace removed photo tiles with 1" photo tiles cut from smaller theme- or subject-related photos.

Float a double-sided photo mosaic

Trudy Sigurdson (Victoria, British Columbia, Canada) takes cutting and reassembling a photo mosaic a step further by mounting the cropped pieces back to back on a page protector. The see-through element of the page protector gives the illusion that the photos are "floating" on the page. Follow the step shots below to create your own floating mosaic image. Remember to design the next page that follows in a way that complements the see-through element.

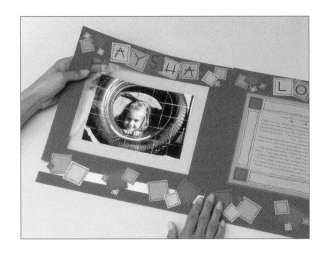

1 Start with two different, yet same-size, photos. Attach strips of temporary adhesive to the back of both photos; adhere back to back to prevent slipping while cropping. Use a craft knife and metal straightedge ruler to slice photos into 1" wide vertical strips. Then slice the strips horizontally to create 1" photo tiles. Keep tiles in proper order as you crop to make reassembly easier.

2 Cut apart one page protector to create a single sheet. Begin assembling one photo mosaic on the first side of the page protector, beginning in the center and working outward until center row is complete. Flip the page protector over. Begin assembling the second photo mosaic on the second side of the page protector, beginning in the center and working outward until center row is complete.

3 Adhere remaining photo tiles row by row, flipping page over as you go, until double mosaic is complete.

Whenever I hear Dan Fogelberg's song of this title, it reminds me that childhood is fleeting and that we must strive to keep the child within. Charley, I hope you continue to feel the joy that I often see on your seven-year-old face. In keeping with that, I've made a mosaic puzzle for you to play with from now until you're 102! If you get stuck, the guide is under this journaling.
Love, Mom   *October 2002*

Mat a removable mosaic puzzle

How do you tie an element of fun into a photo mosaic? Make it into a removable puzzle as Cindy Wallach (Randolph, New Jersey) did with an enlarged photo of her son. Follow the step shots below to turn a layout into an interactive challenge! Make sure to hide a small intact photo somewhere on the page in case the puzzle needs a little help to be solved.

1 Begin with a matted 8 x 8" photo. Use a wax pencil and graphing ruler to mark three vertical cutting lines 2" apart. Then mark three horizontal cutting lines 2" apart. Finally, draw a diagonal cutting line from corner to corner in each square, all going the same diagonal direction.

2 Hold matted and marked photo on cutting mat with a grid pattern of temporary adhesive to prevent slipping while cropping. Use a craft knife and metal straightedge ruler to cut on all cutting lines. After cuts are made, use a soft cloth to remove any wax pencil residue.

3 Remove mosaic puzzle from cutting mat and place on page in proper order with temporary adhesive to complete. A temporary adhesive will make repeated disassembly and re-assembly of the puzzle easier.

Slice a diamond mosaic

Kelly Angard (Highlands Ranch, Colorado) turned an enlarged photo into an intricately cut geometric mosaic in no time at all with the help of a mosaic template. Follow the step shot below to horizontally slice a photo into diamond shapes and then reassemble. Use the template on a single photo, or combine several photos for even more visual interest.

1 Adhere a temporary adhesive to back of photo. Place photo on plastic foam cutting mat. Layer diamond mosaic template (EZ2Cut Shapemakers by EZ2Cut/Accu-Cut) on top of photo and position template using template's placement guidelines. Holding cutting mat, photo and template firmly in place, slice through template's channels to create diagonal slices. Flip template over. Line up the photo and position template using template's placement guidelines. Slice through template's channels to create diagonal slices in the opposite direction. Reassemble on cardstock.

Piece scraps to form a mosaic scene

Tracy Wynn (Truro, Nova Scotia, Canada) was inspired by a Beatle's album cover which featured a large photo made up of many very small photos to create her own unique work of art. Cut photo scraps into ¼" squares and mount on cardstock into a free-form design. If you prefer, lightly pencil desired design onto background to use as a guideline. Run photo scraps through a Xyron™ and use tweezers for easier assembly.

Create an abstract mosaic

An intricate page full of photo "shards" is creatively assembled together in Kelly Angard's (Highlands Ranch, Colorado) monochromatic mosaic. Using a craft knife and metal straight-edge ruler, cut out large diamond shapes from three enlarged photos that contain focal points for your layout. Mount on background. Randomly cut background pieces into shards in a variety of sizes from photo scraps. Mount pieces in place on your page, leaving a small amount of space between pieces. Run photos through a Xyron™ machine to ease the mounting process and use tweezers for handling small pieces.

Variation 1

Piece together a 3-D mosaic

Kim Rudd (Idledale, Colorado) uses a graduating shape template to create dimensional variations of a photo mosaic. One photo is cut into slices and segments and then reassembled leaving a small amount of space between each piece (variation 1 upper left). The second photo is cut into "L" shapes using the same template (variation 2 below). Reassembly takes a different route by alternately mounting segments with self-adhesive foam spacers for a multidimensional look. Follow the step shots below to create two variations of a dimensional mosaic.

Variation 2

1 For variation 1, adhere a temporary adhesive to back of photo. Place photo on plastic foam cutting mat. Layer nested template (Coluzzle® by Provo Craft) on top of photo and center. Holding cutting mat, photo and template firmly in place, use a craft knife to slice through the desired channels on the template. Remove template and use a metal straightedge ruler and craft knife to slice diagonally from center to outer corners as shown in the following picture.

2 Reassemble mosaic slices onto cardstock, being careful to keep photo slices in proper order and with even spaces between the slices. Use self-adhesive foam spacers to adhere specially selected photo slices for dimension. Cover corner slices with a piece of cut cardstock if desired.

1 For variation 2, follow the first and second steps for variation 1, except make no diagonal cuts. Reassemble sliced mosaic beginning at the center and working outward toward the edges. Use self-adhesive foam spacers to adhere specially selected photo slices for dimension.

montage & collage

Try these fun new takes on photomontage (a collage that is just photos) or a photo collage
(a collage that incorporates photos with other items). Photo themes as broad as the spectrum of
our lives are the perfect medium to use in these techniques.

Integrate color duplicates to form a single montage

Using four copies of the same photo in different tones (two in color, one in sepia and one in black-
and-white), Julie Mullison (Superior, Colorado) gives colored variation to a single image with freehand-cut segments reassembled atop one another. Set aside one of the colored photos as the
background for this design. Using a craft knife, cut the focal point from a duplicate color photo in
a freehand shape and set aside. Cut two more freehand shapes from the sepia and black-and-
white photos. Layer freehand-cut shapes atop one another and then on colored background photo
varying colored tones with each layer. Make sure to line up layers over original images to provide
a multicolored single image.

Assemble an abstract montage

Geometric shaped photo scraps are layered together by Jodi Amidei (Memory Makers) as a free-form background design with visual impact. Geometric photo shapes can be randomly freehand cut, or can be cut to follow a pre-drawn design on background cardstock before layering together. For best results, select thematic photo scraps that provide high contrast when montaged. Photos Kelli Noto (Centennial, Colorado)

Crop a photomontage into a circle

A number of happy faces are silhouette cut and layered in Pamela Frye Hauer's (Denver, Colorado) circle montage. Layer cropped and silhouette-cut photos together on background paper. Cut into circle using a template or plate as a guide. This technique can provide thematic symbolism by cutting into a shape that relates to the photos. Photos Cynthia Anning (Virginia Beach, Virginia)

Assemble a lifetime collage

Valerie Barton's (Flowood, Mississippi)'s oval-cropped photo collage is a fun and successful way to document "then and now" photos in a showcase of lifetime achievements. First, silhouette crop subjects from selected photos. Assemble photos collage-style atop background paper of choice, filling as much space as the size of your oval-shaped template or cutter requires. Adhere photos in place when satisfied with the arrangement. Use oval-shaped template or cutter to cut collage into an oval; mat with cardstock. Accent collage on the left and right with smaller, matted photos of the subject as shown.

Piece together a quilt montage

MaryJo Regier (Memory Makers) pieces together a comforting and symbolic quilt full of peaceful images which reflects the comfort she finds in being a free American. Collect a group of themed photos to crop into shapes. Lightly draw wavy guidelines onto background cardstock; freehand cut photos to fit between drawn guidelines. Make sure to leave a small amount of space between cropped photos when mounting.

Victorian

BEAUTIES

Anne Estelle & Mary Katherine

1904

Form a shapely collage

Pamela Frye Hauer (Denver, Colorado) gives feminine shape to a layered collage of heritage photos. Size and cut out torso pattern on page 123. Layer cropped and silhouette-cut photos over torso shape. Turn over layered shape and trim off photo edges around torso. Embellish with stickers, fabric and jewels as desired.

Create a "handy" collage

We've got to hand it to Holle Wiktorek (Clarksville, Tennessee) for assembling a unique collage symbol that encompasses a rewarding teaching career. Size and silhouette-cut the pattern on page 123 to work with your page. Lay silhouette-cut pattern and photos on a light box to determine desired placement. Mount photo pieces over pattern in a collage-like fashion; trim off edges along pattern. Collect a handful of themed photos to layer into an interesting collage variation.

Silhouette crop an imaginative montage

MaryJo Regier (Memory Makers) captures the many things on her husband's mind with an artistic and imaginative photomontage. Silhouette crop a myriad of images in a variety of sizes and arrange in an eye-pleasing fashion. Leave open space on the page so that the eye will fall on collected images. Use a photo scrap to create a journaling mat for a perfect match. Have fun with this technique and open your mind to its unlimited possibilities!

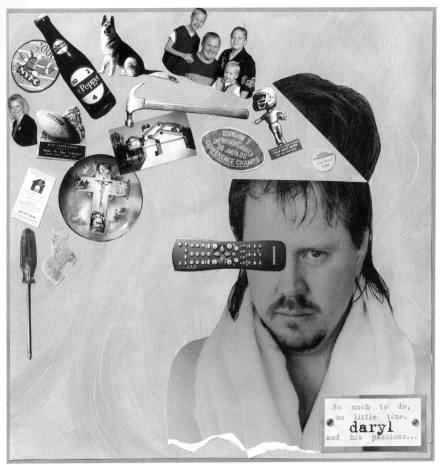

Louis Edward Fitzner

1903–1993

Beloved father, brother, husband, most of all one special grandfather.

Crop a triptych for a montage's focal point

Jill Tennyson (Lafayette, Colorado) pieces together a meaningful tribute with a biographical montage of cropped photos set off by a three-panel "triptych" at the montage's center. Enlarge the pattern on page 123 to fit your page. Silhouette cut pieces to serve as a pattern for your photos. Trace shapes over photos, silhouette cut and assemble as shown.

Cut free-form shapes into travel montage

Julie Mullison (Superior, Colorado) adds an imaginative accent to her travel montage by cutting free-form bird shapes into a handful of layered photos. Slicing shapes into photos breaks up the montage enough to keep the eye from being overwhelmed with layered images. Follow the step shots below to add visual interest to your photos with negative shapes.

1 Assemble and adhere photomontage on cardstock of choice, trimming away any overlap of photos at cardstock edges. If desired, use a wax pencil to freehand draw birds in flight before cutting or use a craft knife to cut them freehand from the photos—cutting through photos and cardstock. Discard negative bird pieces or use them as a page embellishment.

movables

What could be more fun than "moving" photos? From spinning and hinged-door photos to photo bobbleheads, animal cut-outs, slides, wheels and dissolving scenes, these animated cropping techniques are sure to propel your scissors into full motion!

Twirl a pinwheel

Jodi Amidei (Memory Makers) crafts a fanciful pinwheel that is easier to make than it looks. Photocopy pattern on page 123, enlarging until pattern is 4" square. Follow the step shots below to slice and fold your own photo pinwheel. Use colorful photos with complementary-colored cardstock or black-and-white photos with colored cardstock for eye-catching contrast.

1 Apply adhesive to back of photo; mount atop lightweight cardstock. Transfer pattern to photo or crop photo into a 4" square. Use a graphing ruler to draw 1½" cutting lines perpendicular to square corners as shown; cut on lines to form pinwheel "blades." Punch a ⅛" hole in the center of square.

2 One at a time, fold or curl pinwheel blades in toward center of the pinwheel, secure in place with glue dot adhesive. When all blades are securely in place, add brad fastener at the center of the pinwheel.

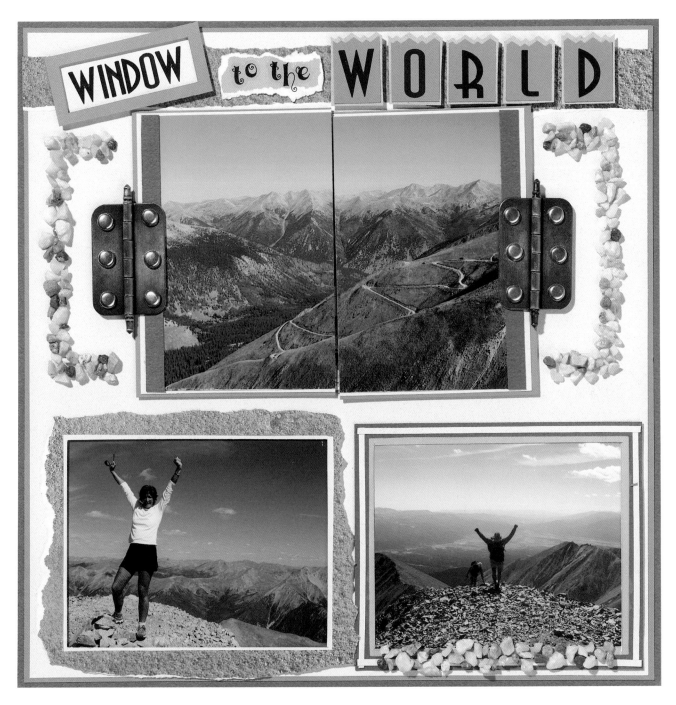

Assemble a hinged door

Hinged photo "doors" open up to reveal Kelly Angard's (Highlands Ranch, Colorado) breathtaking view from the top of one of Colorado's 14,000-foot mountains. Photo "doors" are created from an enlarged double matted photo sliced vertically down the middle. Mount hinges on each photo door and to the page with brad fasteners for a secure hold. Place hinge on one side of photo door and mark holes with a pencil; set hinge aside. Pierce holes with paper piercer or craft knife; secure hinge to photo door with brad. Lay photo door with attached hinge on page; follow the above steps to secure doors to page.

Adam was so excited when you were born because you share the same birthday. You are exactly 17 years apart. For the past two years of your life he's been in Uruguay so he's missed getting to share birthdays when you were old enough to understand what that meant. Even during our visit when we tried to explain it you asked him "did you had a Mini Mouse cake too?"

Add hardware hinges to a photo window

Matted photo doors secured with hardware hinges open to reveal one of Brandi Ginn's (Lafayette, Colorado) favorite family portraits. Follow the step shots below to assemble peek-a-boo photo panels. Landscape or textile photos are a good choice to use as framing images for photo panels.

1 Use an oval shape cutter (Shaping Memories) to crop oval "peek-a-boo door" into top photo. Place cutter directly on photo at center and adjust to the desired size following manufacturer's instructions. Hold photo and cutter firmly to ensure precision cutting. To cut with a template, position template atop photo at center. Trace oval outline with a wax pencil. Cut a slit in center of oval with a craft knife; insert scissors to cut out oval. Discard resulting oval; slice oval frame vertically down center to create door panels.

2 Mat door panels with cardstock. Mount "peek-a-boo photo" on cardstock trimmed to the same length and width as the matted door panels. Mount hinges using Terrifically Tacky Tape (Art Accents) or glue dots, tucking adhesive-laden hinge behind cardstock so it won't show.

Create a photo bobblehead

Kelly Angard (Highlands Ranch, Colorado) adds "character" to photo characters with a movable, silhouette-cut bobblehead. Follow the step shots below to add interactive fun to your own cast of characters with a little bit of coiled wire. Try this easy technique with photos of animals or favorite family members with a good sense of humor!

1 Start with two same-sized photo enlargements. Silhouette-crop subject (in this case, Pooh and children) from first photo; set aside. Silhouette-crop photo subject that you wish to "bobble" (in this case, Pooh's head) from second photo. Trace head onto foam core board and cut out with a craft knife, cutting ⅛" inside your traced lines. Mount cropped photo on cropped foam core.

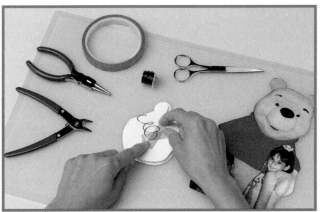

2 To create bobblehead, attach a 2½" coil of heavy-gauge wire to back of foam core using Terrifically Tacky Tape (Art Accents). In the same manner, mount bobblehead atop first photo, placing atop its position in the original photo.

Give movement to animal silhouettes

Looking for a new idea for zoo photos? MaryJo Regier (Memory Makers) transforms silhouette-cut animal photos into movable elements by reassembling body parts with small brads. Start with one photo and a duplicate; silhouette cut body from one photo, and legs, tail and head from the other photo. Follow the step shot below to reassemble silhouette-cut body parts.

1 To reattach silhouette-cropped legs and head to body, hold the limbs in place atop the body, lining up all markings to get limbs in their original positions. Punch through both photo layers at the same time with a ¹⁄₁₆" round hand punch. Insert a brad fastener in hole, flip photo art over and flatten brad legs. Repeat as needed until all limbs are reattached.

Add a spring-action surprise element

Kelli Noto (Centennial, Colorado) puts a little spring into her page with a springy wire attachment. A simple addition of wire attached to a grounded silhouette cut shape brings an element of action and fun to photo cropping. Follow the step shot below to add kinetic movement to your page.

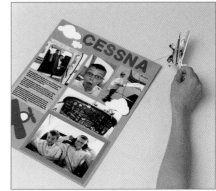

1 Silhouette-crop photo subject (in this case, an airplane) and adhere to one end of Kinetic Wire™ (Kinetic Scrapbooking). Freehand cut a cloud from craft foam and adhere to other end of wire. Leave backing on plane end. Remove backing from cloud end of wire and mount in proper place on page layout. Tuck airplane under another page element when storing.

Integrate slide pulls into photo

Kim Rudd (Idledale, Colorado) integrates movement into her action photos with a crafty slide-pull mechanism. The surfing photo slide pull simulates riding a wave with horizontal movement. Follow the step shots below to add an interactive element to sports or movement-oriented photos.

1 Start with one photo and a duplicate. Freehand draw the slide pull slot on first photo with wax pencil; cut out with craft knife. Slot can be wavy or straight, horizontal or vertical, depending on the photo subject and the movement you wish to create. Use small, sharp scissors to silhouette crop photo subject from second photo (in this case, the surfer).

2 To create the pull-tab slide, cut a 2½ x 4½" rectangle from cardstock. Score rectangle and fold in half. Punch a ¾" circle (Family Treasures) from white cardstock; place atop unfolded rectangle and punch a ⅛" hole through both layers as shown. Insert eyelet through opening in circle and rectangle cardstock; set eyelet (see page 37). Fold rectangle in half and adhere together with eyelet circle on outside.

3 To assemble sliding mechanism, insert white cardstock circle with eyelet into cut slot, leaving cardstock rectangle behind first photo. Sandwich first photo and second photo together and adhere around sides, keeping area near slide-tab pull adhesive free. Mount silhouette-cropped photo subject (the surfer) atop eyelet to complete.

Assemble a photo turning wheel

A photo wheel that showcases eight photos in the space of one is assembled by Jeanne Norman Sarna of Page Additions. A circle-cut window provides the viewing area for changing images with an easy-to-assemble turning wheel. Follow the step shots below to craft a multi-photo turning wheel on your scrapbook page.

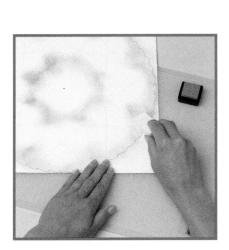

1 If desired, add color to Spin-N-Wheel™ (Page Additions) by blotting stamping ink with a makeup sponge on the spinning wheel's outer edges and inner circle. Use an ink color that is complementary to the photos you will mount on the wheel. Allow drying time. Remove perforated corners of page that hold the wheel; discard.

2 Use the template provided to crop eight photos into circles. Trace template onto each individual photo in desired position; cut out with scissors. Wipe any wax residue from photos with soft cloth.

3 Mount and adhere cropped photos to wheel, using the wheel's preprinted arrows for proper placement and overlapping photos as needed, all going in the same direction. This will prevent the wheel from "catching" on the photos when it is turned. Use a brad fastener to attach wheel to background page provided in kit. Remove adhesive backing from corners of background page and mount cover page. Embellish and accent cover as desired with wheel turn at bottom of page.

Slice a dissolving scene

Jeanne Norman Sarna for Page Additions highlights a "moving" way to transition from one photo image to another with a sliding photo element. A moving, louvered-like window is created using Slide-n-See™ pre-made tabs and sliding wheel which changes a photo image right before your eyes. Follow the step shots on the next page and manufacturer's instructions to add hidden photo images to your scrapbook pages.

Photo 1

Photo 2

1 Start with one duplicate each of two different photos (total of four photos). Use a craft knife and a metal straightedge ruler to crop the four photos into slices, following the diagram and the diagram below. Keep pictures in order. The photo slices that are turned upside down will be discarded.

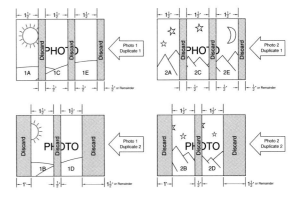

2 Arrange Slide-N-See™ tabs provided in front of you, marked side down, in the order shown at left. Mount and adhere the photo slices from both photo 1s onto the tabs following manufaturer's instructions, making sure to adhere the photo corners well to prevent "catching" when the slide is pulled.

3 Arrange photo slices from photo 2 on the cover slots— partially inserting the photo slices into the cover's slots and leaving approximately 1" of photo still showing. Photo slices should be centered vertically. Adhere photo slices into place, making sure that the adhesive is not on the portion of the photo that extends through the slot.

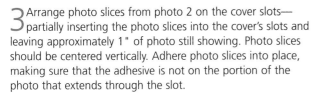

4 Working from the back side of the cover, insert photo tabs photo side down under photo slices—pushing tabs all the way in and then laying them flat against the cover. Each new tab overlaps the previous tab in two places; you will finish with the pull tab. Adhere the overlapping sections in the boxes marked by an X symbol. Adhesive should not overhang the boxes; it may inhibit movement of the sliding mechanism.

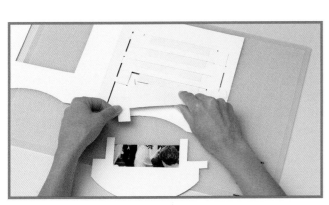

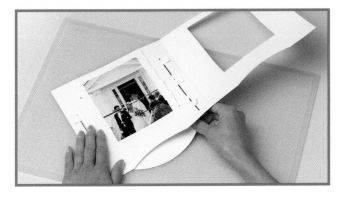

5 Flip cover back over and gently bend each of the five "motion limiting" tabs and insert them through the corresponding slot in the cover. Gently push and pull the pull-tab to test the sliding mechanism. Follow manufacturer's instructions to properly mount the Slide-N-See photo art on a scrapbook page.

additional instructions

Add dimension with well-placed slices (Page 3, Bookplate)

Trudy Sigurdson (Victoria, British Columbia, Canada) gives you the feeling you are really walking out onto this pier. First, start with two duplicates of the same photo. Use a craft knife and a metal straightedge ruler to slice along the lines of the pier on one photo and crop out the horizon from the second photo. On the second photo, slice just below the horizon. Triple mat the second photo. Mount first photo over the top of the original. Use ¼" self-adhesive foam spacers beneath the sliced pier for lift. Use ⅛" self-adhesive foam spacers beneath the sliced horizon line for lift.

Slice and stair-step tri-colored photos (Page 6, Introduction)

A great way to give your photos visual appeal is to "stair step" them while relining up the original image. Add a second twist—each photo slice is a different color! Begin with three 5 x 7" enlargements of the same photo: one in color, one sepia-toned and one black-and-white. Slice each picture into three equal segments with a craft knife and metal straightedge ruler. Choose one cropped photo segment from each of the three photo colors. Cut ½" from bottom of left-side photo. Cut ¼" from top and bottom of center photo. Cut ½" from top of right-side photo. Assemble photos together & mat segments permanently, lining up photo segments to recreate original image. Michele Gerbrandt (Memory Makers)

Photo Credits

Artist Index

patterns

Use these helpful patterns to complete photo-cropping projects featured in this book.
Use a photocopier or scanner to enlarge the patterns as needed to fit your photographs,
then reproduce the patterns.

International female symbol, page 68

Tags, page 52-53

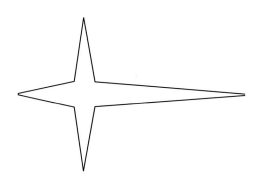

Cross, page 69

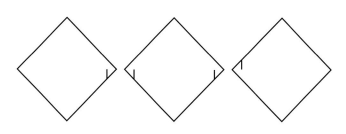

Interlocking photo tiles,
page 74

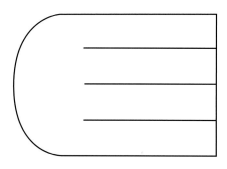

Woven heart, page 86

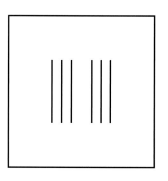

Woven panel A, page 87

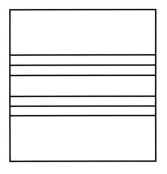

Woven panel B, page 87

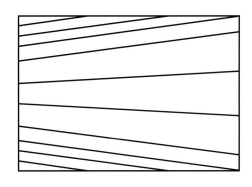

Photo loom, page 88

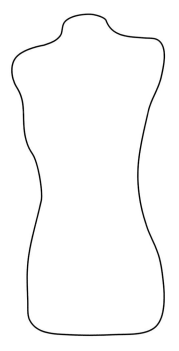

Collage torso, page 106

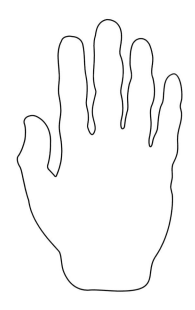

Collage hand, page 107

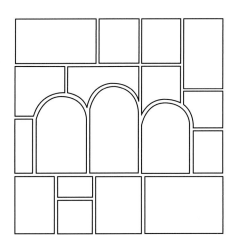

Triptych, page 108

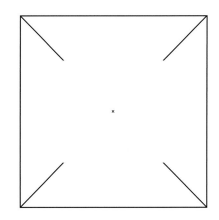

Pinwheel, page 110

glossary of techniques

3-D Photos

Using foam spacers between layers of photos to add depth and dimension can create 3-D photo art. See pages 3, 42, 58, 71, 85, 101, 113.

Borders

Photo borders put all of those leftover photo trimmings and snippets to use. Or, make great use of extra people shots, mini studio portrait shots and extra travel photos by creating interesting photo page borders. See pages 74, 81.

Collage

Collage is a collection of different photographs adhered together on a page and usually includes other embellishments or craft supplies. The elements may or may not overlap. See pages 102-109.

Cropping

Traditionally, cropping means cutting or trimming a photo to keep only the most important parts of the image. This book gives creative cropping a whole new meaning, however, with a multitude of ideas, tips and techniques for using every bit of a cropped photo. See pages 12-119.

Digital

A computer-related term for the process of using numerical digits to create uniform photographic images as shot with a digital camera or scanned into a computer with a scanner and saved on and retrieved from a CD-ROM. See page 10.

Frames

Cropping frames into photos is an easy way to add class to your photos without taking attention away from the photo's subject, and the framing variations are many. See pages 34-43.

Illusions

Creating photo illusions through creative photo cropping extends the imagery of a conventional photograph. The trickery of photo illusions can exaggerate size and scale, pair unlikely photo subjects for interesting, comical effects or play upon dimension and light. See page 67 and pages 111-119 of *Memory Makers Creative Photo Cropping for Scrapbooks.*

Interlocking

Interlocking is a cropping technique used to tuck slices of a photo into itself or to join different photos together. See pages 29 and 74.

Letters, Numbers & Symbols

Another fun variation of shape cropping is cutting your photos into letters, numbers and widely recognized symbols. Many templates are available for this use. We've provided examples of freehand-cut designs to inspire you as well. See pages 60-69.

Mats

This cropping technique accents the photo layered beneath the mat and makes a great use of photos that might otherwise go unused. See pages 34-43.

Mosaics

Pieced photo mosaics are a captivating way to display photos, whether you are cropping and reassembling a single photo or combining several photos. Photo mosaics are as diverse as the photos you use, each lending its own fresh originality to the finished design. See pages 92-101.

Movables

What could be more fun than "moving" photos? From spinning and hinged-door photos to movable bobble-heads, slides, wheels and dissolving scenes, these animated cropping techniques are easier than they look! See pages 75 and 110-119.

GOD BLESS AMERICA

Nobody knows what a boy is worth
We'll have to wait and see
But every man in a noble place
A boy once used to be.

Anonymous

Photomontage

Montage is similar to collage, but the pictures or parts of pictures are superimposed or overlapped so that they form a blended whole. Photomontages are made of strictly photos, with no other scrapbook embellishments. See pages 102-109.

Punches

Discover the versatility and ease of using punches to crop photos. With so many different punches on the market today, photo-cropping possibilities are as limitless as your imagination. See pages 70-81.

Reverse-Image

Reverse-image photos are useful when a mirrored photo effect is desired. To obtain a reverse-image reprint of your original photo, the photo print operator should flip the negative so that the emulsion side is opposite of the correct printing method normally used. Request that the original image and the reversed image are an exact match. See pages 27 and 66.

Shapes

Whether freehand cut or cropped with the use of a template, shape cropping adds simple style to scrapbook theme pages while narrowing the focus of the photo's subject. See pages 50-81.

Silhouettes

One of the most popular cropping techniques, silhouette cropping requires you to trim around the contours of the figures in your photos. For added interest, experiment with partial silhouetting to add a whole new dimension to page design. See pages 19, 38, 40, 85, 94.

Slicing

Slicing usually involves cropping a photo into slices or segments either freehand or using a craft knife and metal straightedge ruler. Slicing can be horizontal, vertical, straight, wavy or random. See pages 6 and 14-33.

Tearing

Tearing is fairly new to the photo cropping scene. It's a great way to add drama or soften photos. Remove the clear plastic backing from a photo to make tearing easier. Tear slowly to stay in control of the tear's direction. See pages 44-49.

Weaving

Cropping and weaving two copies of the same photo together, one in color and one in black-and-white, is a unique and highly visual technique that works great with any photo subject and any photo size. See pages 84-91.

sources

The following companies manufacture products featured in this book. Please check your local retailers to find these materials. In addition, we have made every attempt to properly credit the items mentioned in this book. We apologize to any company that we have listed incorrectly or the sources were unknown, and we would appreciate hearing from you.

3L Corp.
(800) 828-3130
www.3lcorp.com

3M Stationary
(800) 364-3577
www.3m.com

Accu-Cut®
1-800-288-1670
www.accucut.com

American Tombow, Inc.
(800) 835-3232
www.tombowusa.com

Art Accents
(360) 733-8989
www.artaccents.net

Carl Mfg. USA, Inc.
(800) 257-4771
www.carl-products.com

C-Thru® Ruler Company, The
(800) 243-8419
(wholesale only)
www.cthruruler.com

Centis
www.centis.com

Eastman Kodak Company
www.kodak.com

Ecstasy Crafts
(888) 288-7131
www.ecstasycrafts.com

EK Success™ Ltd.
(800) 524-1349
www.eksuccess.com

Emagination Crafts, Inc.
(630) 833-9521
www.emaginationcrafts.com

Epson America, Inc. www.epson.com

Excel Hobby Blade Corporation
(800) 845-2770
www.exceltools.net

EZ2Cut Templates
(800) 288-1670
www.ez2cut.com

Family Treasures, Inc.®
(800) 413-2645
www.familytreasures.com

Fiskars, Inc.
(800) 950-0203
www.fiskars.com

Fredrix Artist Canvas
www.fredrixartistcanvas.com

Glue Dots® International (wholesale only)
(888) 688-7131
www.gluedots.com

Hermafix (see Centis)

If you love to learn new scrapbook techniques, you won't want to miss these best-selling Memory Makers books!

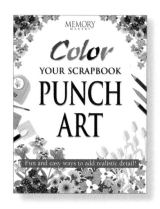

Highsmith®
(800) 558-2110
www.highsmith.com

Hot Off The Press, Inc.
(800) 227-9595
www.craftpizazz.com

Hoyle Products, Inc.
(800) 345-1950
www.hoylegrips.com

Incire™
www.incire.com

Kinetic Scrapbooking
(800) 893-0639
www.kineticscrapbooking.com

Martha Stewart
(800) 950-7130
www.marthastewart.com

Nankong Enterprises, Inc.
(302) 731-2995
www.nankong.com

Page Additions™
(248) 813-8888
www.pageadditions.com

Photographic Solutions, Inc.
(508) 759-2322
www.photographicsolutions.com

Pioneer Photo Albums®, Inc.
(800) 366-3686
pioneer@pioneerphotoalbums.com

Provo Craft®
(888) 577-3545
www.provocraft.com

Ranger Industries, Inc.
(800) 244-2211
www.rangerink.com

Scrapbook Magic
(763) 560-9970
www.scrapbookmagic.net

Shaping Memories
(636) 390-8529
www.shapingmemories.com

Speedball Art Products Company
(800) 898-7224
www.speedballart.com

Stamping Station Inc.
(801) 444-3828
www.stampingstation.com

Stamporium
(800) 398-6260 (orders only)
www.stamporium.com

Un-du® Products, Inc.
(888) 289-8638
www.un-du.com

U.S. Shell, Inc.
(956) 554-4500
www.usshell.com

Xyron™, Inc.
(800) 793-3523
www.xyron.com

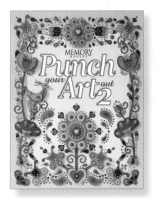

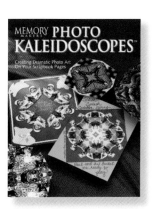

index